Taking Charge of Your Life

(Originally published under the
title *Character Building*)

By Ernest Wood

*This publication made possible with
the assistance of the Kern Foundation*

The Theosophical Publishing House
Wheaton, Ill. U.S.A.
Madras, India/London, England

The Theosophical Publishing House
306 West Geneva Road
Wheaton, Illinois 60189

A publication of the Theosophical Publishing House,
a department of the Theosophical Society in America.

Library of Congress Cataloging in Publication Data

Wood, Ernest, 1883-1965
    Taking charge of your life.

    (A Quest book)
    "Formerly published under the title: Character
building."
    1. Character.   2. Conduct of life.   I. Wood, Ernest,
1883-1965. Character building.   II. Title
BJ1521.W65   1985   299'.934   84-40512
ISBN 0-8356-0594-9 (pbk.)

Printed in the United States of America

Cover design by *Jane A. Evans*

Contents

Foreword

It matters not how strait the gate,
How charged with punishments the scroll,
I am the master of my fate;
I am the captain of my soul.

The poet William Ernest Henley's belief in the indomitable human spirit, as expressed in his poem "Invictus," is unfashionable in much modern literature, but it is echoed in William Faulkner's acceptance speech for the Nobel Prize:

I decline to accept the end of man. It is easy enough to say that man is immortal simply because he will endure. . . . I refuse to accept this. I believe that man will not merely endure: he will prevail.

Humanity will prevail because each human being can say, "I am the master of my fate." Whatever the origin myths of the world's religions say about the creation of men and women, all individuals create themselves.

Two of the great, and complementary, principles of theosophical thought are *karma*, the concept that moral law rules all of life, guaranteeing that we get what we have deserved, and *free will*, the concept that we can nevertheless take charge of our lives, so that we need not be stuck with what we are now, but can make of ourselves whatever we want to be. You *can* take charge of your life! That is the promise of this book.

The author outlines a program for self-development, with steps that are structured so that readers can systematically work on themselves. It includes exercises by which we can learn to master our fate and captain our soul—it tells us how we can take charge of our own lives, through the art of character building.

What is this thing called "character" and why should we want to build it?

A friend of mine had a teen-aged daughter, who was something of a trial to her father. One day he lost his temper and lectured her severely about her faults. When he paused for breath, she looked at him with great, wide eyes and asked, "Daddy, what do you suppose makes me act this way—heredity or environment?" Her message was clear. In either case she held her father responsible for her character.

Most parents, observing their offspring, quickly decide that heredity and environment alone are not enough to account for how children behave, that parents are not solely responsible. There has to be something else. And there is.

To be sure, each of us has a heredity from our biological parents, genes that determine a great deal about us—the color of our eyes, the curliness of our hair, a tendency to asthma, and so on. We are also greatly influenced by the surroundings in which we grow up. Our environment strongly influences our inclination to be mechanical or bookish, to be afraid of heights or to love them, to feel secure or threatened. Nature and nurture both shape us. But they are not everything. There is something else.

Each of us has a core that is uniquely us. That core interacts with what we inherit from our parents, and it is also affected by our surroundings. But that core is not the result of heredity or environment. It is something we bring to our birth and something we live with throughout our alloted years. It is our character.

Our character is the third factor in our lives. It interacts with our heredity and our environment in complex ways. It makes us ourselves. We are more than a temporary unit in a biological process by which the genes reproduce themselves. We are more than the accidental product of environmental forces that blow like the winds of a sirocco, shaping the dust it passes over. Each of us has an individual character which is more than the by-product of other forces. We are our character, and it is truly us.

Our character did not evolve in just the present lifetime. In the theosophical view from which Ernest Wood wrote his study of character building, all of us live, not just once on this earth, but many times. We each have behind us a string of lives, of births and deaths, stretching back into the mists of time. And each of us will continue for a long while into the future to be reborn, time after time, in one spot or another on this globe, into various cultures and ways of living. There is an eventual end to the cycle of births and deaths; but for most of us, that end is a long way off. What we need to do now is learn how to live well in this life in which we find ourselves.

We cannot do much about our heredity and environment—nothing whatever about the first and very little about the second, especially about the environment of our earliest years, which seems to be crucial in shaping our personality. But we are not just automata, conditioned by our genes and our training. We are also individuals. Free individuals. We are not just passive instruments, harps strung by our ancestors and played upon by the unpredictable winds of our surroundings. We can respond at will.

What enables us to respond to our ancestry and to the world about us is our character. In turn, the kind of response we make creates for us day by day a new character. For character is not fixed, but fluid. By the decisions we make today, we create tomorrow's self. Thus the kind of response we make to life is ultimately more important than either our heredity or our environment. We are that response. It marks the area in which we have exercised our free will, in which we are truly ourselves.

We have borrowed the word *character* ultimately from Greek, where it meant 'an engraved mark or brand.' That old history of the word tells us something important about the thing it names. Character is what we engrave upon ourselves. It is the mark of our individuality. Our individuality, also called our "higher" self, is the link between the personalities of our various lives. In each new life, the "higher" self sends forth the accumulated character we have built up during past lives to become the core of the new personality.

Life after life we go on building our character, for it is by no means the product of a single existence. It is true that the personalities of each of our lives do not survive those life cycles. All the evanescent qualities that go to make up the masks of our personalities are lost with each death: our names, our appearance, our passing preferences, our little quirks all dissipate. What remain, however, are certain abiding tendencies, certain persevering qualities, that emerge in the next personality. What remains is our character.

The character developed in one life is the seed that is planted; it sprouts in a future heredity and is fostered by the environment of a new life. Our character is the part of ourselves we can most directly control, and in controlling it, we control our present and our future. In building our character, we are building not only for this life, but for many lives to come. We are taking charge of our lives.

Thus character is what we really are, and building character is ultimately all we do in life. The question is not whether we ought to or will build character. We do so every day in every decision we make, and in every action we take, in every word we say, in every thought we have. We can't escape character building. To live is to create character. The only question is whether we shall be aware of what we are doing. We usually go through life building character unconsciously. Shall we build it consciously for a change? That is the question Ernest Wood puts to us in this little book.

Ernest Wood (1883-1965) was born in Manchester, England, but spent nearly forty years of his adult life studying and teaching in India. He was an educator, the founder of several Indian colleges affiliated with the Universities of Bombay and Madras, and wrote more than thirty books on such subjects as yoga, mind training, oriental philosophy, and practical citizenship. He traveled many times around the world, lecturing on philosophy, psychology, and theosophy. He served as International Secretary of the Theosophical Society during the presidency of Annie Besant. He was, in the best sense, a theosophist in both theory and practice.

Wood approaches his subject in two main ways: first, by an extended metaphor in which he likens building character to building a house—a bungalow of the Indian type, with a verandah for protection from the sun and a garden and an orchard around it. In this metaphor (developed in chapters 3-10), he focuses especially on the three virtues of courage, truth, and love, which he considers to be fundamental. Wood did not choose those three at random. They correspond to the three aspects of our individuality or "higher" self, called in the theosophical tradition will, wisdom, and activity, and also to the three aspects of the ultimate reality, called Being, Awareness, and Bliss (in Sanskrit, *sat, chit, ananda*). Wood does not make these analogies explicit in his book, but they are clearly present for anyone to find.

Wood's second approach to the subject of character building (developed in chapters 11-18) stresses the inherent direction already present in each of us. In a sense, the building of character is a process by which we become actually what we already are potentially—like an oak tree growing out of an acorn. We all have our own inner nature, which it is our calling in life to realize and fulfill. In India it is called *dharma,* the ultimate law of our nature. We are each inwardly laws to ourselves.

Although we are each unique, we (and, for that matter, everything else in the universe) can also be classified into one of seven types. In theosophical terms, everyone belongs to one of seven "rays." Wood personifies the seven human types of temperament: the person of will, the philanthropist, the philosopher, the magician, the scientist, the devotee, and the artist. Each of these seven types has distinct characteristics and relates to the world accordingly. Readers can try to discover their ray from Wood's brief sketches of the seven types, and so go about character building appropriately.

These two approaches to character building by no means exhaust what Wood has to say on the subject. Toward the end of his book, in a reference to the epic story of Yudhishtira, he focuses on a very important point—that we must make use of both our strengths and our weaknesses, our virtues and our vices. Out of our greatest weaknesses can come our greatest strengths.

The same point is made in the theosophical classic *Light on the Path*, whose rule 20 is concerned with the "ladder" by which we mount from our past to our future.

> All steps are necessary to make up the ladder. The vices of man become steps in the ladder, one by one, as they are surmounted. The virtues of man are steps indeed, necessary—not by any means to be dispensed with. Yet, though they create a fair atmosphere and a happy future, they are useless if they stand alone. The whole nature of man must be used wisely by the one who desires to enter the way.

That sums up the central message in Ernest Wood's book on character building. We must use our whole nature wisely: body and soul, vices and virtues. Our character is what we are, and we are a natural whole.

There are many useful works on the building of

character, for example, the chapter of that name in Annie Besant's book *In the Outer Court.* But Ernest Wood's study is an especially good introduction to the subject—clear, like everything he wrote, and perceptive. In the new edition the editor has pruned from the original, references and illustrations that are no longer suitable and substituted a few that are more timely and has brought the presentation up to date in various ways, while scrupulously retaining the flavor of Wood's prose. The editing has been what Ernest Wood himself would surely have done, had he had the opportunity. All readers of this new edition can be grateful to Quest Books for making it once more available.

John Algeo

I

Your Real Self

1
WHY BUILD CHARACTER?

Why should you deliberately aim at the development of character? First, because you will never be satisfied or happy till you do, and second, because the game of life requires it of you as a duty. You are alive for a purpose, and somewhere within your consciousness you have a dim inkling of that fact; you are either seeking or expecting something the lack of which leaves you without complete satisfaction. Your procession of little destinies—from tomorrow to next week, to next year, and to the end of life in this body—and your larger destiny to be fulfilled in unimaginable greatness in the future beyond that (in the course of rebirths on earth and life in other worlds) all lie in your own hands. The coming of that greatness may now be accelerated by the efforts that you make, just as your present condition has resulted from efforts that you have made in the past—by no other thing.

No one can eat, learn, feel, or think for you, nor develop your will power or any other part of your character, though you may find environment a source of help or difficulty in your growth. As the power within a tiny seed determines the form, even to a detail, of the mightiest tree, so is the power within you a mere seed of what shall be truly a human and even a god. As no one can grow an oak tree from a mango seed, so nothing in your environment can make you grow into something that you are not destined to be.

There is something marvelous in the power within a seed. When that seed is the human soul containing the powers of will, thought, and love, no one should dare to measure its possibilities by a puny and undeveloped imagination. With such powers within, you must not depend upon external accidents for the food, water, and sunshine necessary for your unstunted growth—it is for you to be your own gardener, to understand your own destiny, and to make your circumstances assist you in swift achievement.

It has been determined by your inmost self that you shall develop character, the powers of the soul, through effort and experience. The quantity as well as the quality of your conscious life shall thus ever increase, until it is too great for human limits.

Abundant life is not chiefly to be found, how-

4

ever, in material quantity. You do not need enormous physical riches, any more than you want a huge body, like a giant in a story book; but you do desire abounding *health*, physically, emotionally, and mentally, for these are the spiritual riches of freedom, love, and truth. The spirit within measures its things by quality, not by quantity. What will give you permanent joy is not greater wealth nor power over others, nor the spread of your meaningless name in what people call fame, not longer bones and more abundant flesh, but more character—realization of freedom, love, and truth in all their ramifications and modifications.

For those who aim at these things success is certain, for the power within the seed is on their side; those who aim otherwise have their life forces sapped by a constant struggle to hold what is perishing. And there is always this help, that what you have attained in character will soon reflect itself in your outer life. Material opportunities of all kinds will soon come to those who have determined to make the right use of their powers. Each thing that comes before them will be more significant and more useful to these individuals than it would be to others. Life is a matter of degree, and there is as much difference between one person and another as there is between a horse and the earthworm that is blind and deaf. The external world is also different for each of these. Character deals with circumstances and in the long run makes its own opportunities.

In the course of life, your character undergoes constant modification. Every experience adds something of strength, insight, or feeling. Every feeling and thought, however transient, makes its permanent mark in the growing character. But, as environment plays upon us, there is no such thing as the passive reception of modification in consciousness. The mark that is made in the character by any experience is a compound of two distinct things—the outer event and the inner character that meets it. The result of the reaction between these two (which we may call an experience) produces two effects—a modification in the character of the person and some change in the outer world.

It is the modification within, not the effect in the outer world, that we have to consider in our present study. You and I may go for a sea voyage, be wrecked in the same vessel, and be rescued from the same boat. We may have had the same hunger and thirst and buffeting and fatigue. But, believe me, our experiences have been widely different, because of the difference of character within. One of us may have gained much more benefit than the other—more, that is, of strength or understanding or love built into the character, or rather brought out into it from within the soul as a permanent gain.

Life has never been and cannot be passive, and the growth in character of a human being will be swift or slow, exactly according to what is put forth from within. This generally means effort—effort to act, to understand, to love; effort of working, of thinking, of devotion, or whatever it may be. To be passive is to be dead or asleep for the moment. Even in that religious devotion to God which has been practiced by the most notable saints, there was a constant active effort to open the mind and heart in devotion in order to be conscious of the spiritual force or grace that cannot flow into the closed minds of lazy, thoughtless, and selfish men. Even in this extreme case, there is no real passivity. Rather, a positive, active character is experiencing a modification when it blends within its own being with what, for want of better expression, must be called a downflow of spiritual force.

What is in the heart of the seed, in the depths of the soul, beyond anything that we are able to define as the character of man? We can at present know little about this mystery. For all practical purposes it is character that is the person, and the soul powers become known to us only when they appear in that. It is the character that is the person, and the only thing that can be called progress for anyone is its development.

Life will give you no permanent happiness until you recognize and obey this truth, and realize that life is for the development of character towards a destiny glorious beyond all present imaginings. A spiritual hunger will give you no rest but will drive you on to this goal of human life. Success will follow success as you develop character in the material world, but ever new realms to conquer will open their vistas before you, and spiritual hunger will drive you on till you obtain the greatest fruit of life that human experience can grow, and beyond that something greater still.

It is human destiny to achieve happiness, not by the method of forgetfulness, like the sheep in the meadows that enjoy their simple pleasures and do not think of past or future, but by the method of will, understanding of life, and love, as beings cooperating with God in the work of evolution. We cannot go back and become sheep; it is ours to go forward by our own will power and become gods.

Glance over the world of human endeavor and ask the question, What is it for? Ever since the human form appeared on earth, men have worked with their brains and hands and with infinite labor have turned over the dust of the ground. They have scratched the surface of the earth, gathered stone and iron, built cities and monuments, constructed languages and policies. All these have endured for a space, and then gone forever. But ancient Greece, Rome, Chaldea, Peru, Egypt, and India live now in us. Their material triumphs have turned to dust; their original languages are dead; but all the gain of character that was achieved by those ancient labors is ours now and forever. It is not the work that matters but the workers, individually and collectively. All that exists does so, as an ancient Indian writing says, for the sake of the soul or the self within. Character is the most important thing, and the development of character is the important work.

The world is but a school for all of us, but it is not a cramming institution. In it games play perhaps the greatest part, and most of its objects are merely educative toys, however seriously grown-up people may regard them. Even knowledge is not valuable for its quantity but only for its appositeness to the needs of your character or mine, as leading us to a realization of the truth about life.

I knew a young man who had a great thirst for knowledge; and it was his habit to frequent a large reference library and study all kinds of subjects, in each of which he found absorbing interest. But after a while he grew despondent, for he realized that he could not gather the treasures even of this one library in less than four hundred whole lifetimes of close reading, for there were some half a million volumes in that library alone. That little calculation taught him that it was not the business of life to acquire knowledge, except what is necessary in order that each of us may live truly, kindly, and actively.

The toys of knowledge are endless in their variety, but realization of the truth comes through the use of our powers of thought upon that bit of the world that happens to be ours, and through living a life of love and activity according to that thought. Thinking about life is not living, and the thought that does not find some positive use in my definite scheme of life is not of great benefit to me.

We all have our daily destiny to fulfill; certain knowledge is very important for us. It is wise for us to seek the knowledge that we can best apply to our own life and to concentrate our mental power upon it, so that, like the fabled swan of the Hindus, we may separate the milk of wisdom from the waters of knowledge. I have known little boys to boast that they had walked through every street of their particular town. I have known travelers, or rather tourists, to rush on wheels through every celebrated country of the world; but I am sure that those have learned the lesson of life better who have pursued their quiet occupations and moved abroad occasionally as a corrective and a change. A realization of the truth about life may be found everywhere, and the means to its attainment (the very purpose of life) is indicated in that coarse old proverb that a fool cannot learn from a wise man, but a wise man can learn even from a fool.

Again, the lessons of the school of life do not result in accumulated texts of knowledge, but in character—in what we *are*. For business or social purposes, I may learn Chinese or Latin today. I shall not want those languages forever, but what I have gained in power by learning and using them will be mine for good. It is not accumulated experience that is of use in life—it is experience digested into character. Just as millions of details exist in our memory in some unimaginable unity, so does all our past thinking and willing appear in the sudden decision that we may make today. To each one of us there will come a day when the character within has reached a point of predominance at which we will suddenly say: I *realize* that my destiny is in my own hands, and from this moment forward I will guide my life swiftly and surely to the appointed end of perfection.

Another pointer to the fact that we human beings are required to work out our own destiny is to be seen in our substitution of work and knowledge for the natural protection and instinct that we find in the lower kingdoms of nature. Animals are provided by nature with clothing for purposes of warmth, protection, beauty, and camouflage. Man alone is at the mercy of cold and heat, wind and rain, friends and enemies. But each animal is confined within certain climatic limits and other conditions, outside of which it would be in danger of extinction from heat or cold or enemies; while enlightened man makes his own clothing. The reward of his effort is that his freedom extends from the poles to the equator, as he can adapt his covering to all climates.

We civilized people, weak in proportion to our size, without natural weapons or protective covering, outclassed in all our senses and physical powers by various birds, animals, fishes, and insects, can yet achieve more than any other creature. We can see the minute by means of our microscope; hear the walking of a fly as though it were the galloping of a horse over a hard road by means of our microphone; see what is distant by telescope; travel faster than any animal on earth on our railways and automobiles; speed across the ocean against contrary winds and also travel in its depths; fly higher and swifter than any bird; handle, construct, and control tools, machines, and engines and the powers of water, gas, and electricity; communicate our ideas by means of a code of words; transmit our thoughts over the world by means of telephone, telegraph, and radio; make marvelous calculations by computers, and do many other things far beyond the reach of any other being in the physical world—and all this by virtue of our character. All this we can do because humankind has been put at a disadvantage, which has induced us to develop our character—because, in other words, it is our business to take our destiny into our own hands.

The time will come when those who now achieve their triumphs in wood and brass and iron will learn, as the Indian yogis have long taught us, that there is another field of still greater achievement within the human mind, where powers can be developed beyond anything attainable with external means. No doubt, even in the material world man will soon achieve greater triumphs than those of the present. "Everything," said a philosopher, "becomes fluid to thought," and most probably in the course of time it will be in the power of some of us to remove the Himalayas from their seats and place them elsewhere if we wish. We are only at the ABC of human power. All the forces that we use will presently be found to be feeble beside the powers in the soul.

2
WHAT IS CHARACTER?

Character is the stamp or mark of the soul expressed in life. Meditate for a moment upon your place
in the series of events that we call life, and you will
find that every impulse that comes from the outer
world is dealt with by that inner self who feels and
thinks (however briefly) about it and then forms a
decision that passes into action. Thus the inner
person has exerted some directive influence upon
the flow of events in the outer world. Things are
different because thay have passed through him.

You may divide your life into two parts—an inner self who holds his own balance while he feels,
thinks and acts; and an outer world, including the
body with all its demands and needs. In the life of a
stone the outer is all, so far as we are able to see.
Many plants show a little character, animals more.
Most people show character now and then, but it is

the enlightened ones, in whom the inner life is ruler of the body and environment, adapting all circumstances to an inner purpose, whom we may rightly call persons of character—who are great inside, in whom soul force is greater than the force of bodily habit and environment. Such character will make itself apparent in all the little incidents of life, whether one is living from day to day without a plan but according to set principles, as many people of character do, or is working for a definite goal of achievement. To sum up—a person of character *lives from within* and makes a mark upon his little world, and is therefore both great and good.

Examples of people of character can be found in every walk of life. Thousands of historical and contemporary names could be cited, but for every one whose name has become popularly known there are hundreds of others, equally great and almost as great, who have fought their battles of love and thought and action away from the public gaze, often with nothing to show outside. Such are many of those who have sacrificed the ease and comfort of life to pursue their ideals—the young writer who feels within her the beauty of literature and poetry and would rather starve in a garret with her muse than live in comfort without it; the storekeeper, honest under difficulties; the lawyer, truthful in the face of temptation; the inventor, who gives time and money, and often limb and life, in devotion to his high idea. All of these have had a glimpse within their own soul of some great possibility and have become a devotee to that.

Think, for example, of the pioneers who devoted themselves to the achievement of human flight. All the earlier experimenters sacrificed comfort and safety, and one after another met with serious injury or cruel death in the course of their experiments. Worse than this, they had to face the ridicule of their fellow men—learned and ignorant alike. But they held to their ideal and kept their balance through all these trials, and at last succeeded in giving to mankind the airplane, which has played such a great part for good and ill in the history of mankind.

Or think of the life story of Prince Gautama, who became the Buddha, "who made our Asia mild." As a young man he was surrounded with everything that men desire. He had a loving and beautiful wife, splendid palaces and gardens, good health and intelligence, prospects of lordship over a prosperous and contented kingdom to be handed down by a devoted father. But on several occasions he happened to witness scenes of suffering, disease, and death; and this sorrow of others sank deep into his soul and sent him forth to seek its cause and the means by which it might cease. Such was his spiritual insight that he *knew* by unquestionable and unsilenceable intuition that there must be a solution to the problem of human misery. This concern would not let him, like an ordinary man, sink down before the difficulty and accept the apparently inevitable with a shrug of regret and helplessness, determined only to shield from sorrow those near and dear to himself as far as might be. It was the spiritual vision of the sure triumph of right over all wrong and of man over all sorrow that led him to renounce all comforts and pleasures and material security that stood in the way of his search for enlightenment. He sought in the outer field of nature by his wanderings, and in the depth of his own soul by unyielding meditation, and his search resulted in the Buddhist religion, which today comforts and guides millions.

Such is the loyalty that you must render to the soul within, dimly as you may perceive its longings in those early days of its ascendancy.

What comes out of the soul must be good as well as great, for inside that sanctuary, understanding, will, and love, all work together for a common end. All truly human life is great and good. It is when we forget ourselves (and become predatory animals plus human knowledge) that greatness and goodness leave us, whatever noise we may make in the world. Napoleon was a man of character—not always, but in spasms—but on account of his frequent forgetfulness his greatness and goodness deserted him and ruined his career. If he had not forgotten himself, his genius might have brought him to the front in another way and made him one of the greatest benefactors of the human race.

Nothing can be more important at the beginning of a practical course in the building of character than a firm resolution to look for the light within. We must then try to obey that light when it is recognized, even in the face of grave difficulty.

A great number of people are desperately anxious about comparatively unimportant things but care little for the welfare of the eternal self. Because of this habit, their lives are full of anxiety, and they have lost faith in the truth that if they sought first the will of the self within, the less important outer things would come within their reach when necessary for inner purposes and for the fulfilment of their duty in the world.

• Exercise 1—First Week

Sit down for fifteen to thirty minutes each day to dwell contemplatively on the elements of your daily life. Consider which of your actions were done as the result of material desires—for food, clothing, shelter, amusement or enjoyment, physical, emotional, and mental—and which for spiritual desires, otherwise called ideals—for freedom, love, or understanding, in pursuit of harmony, truth, goodness, or beauty. Try to realize the distinction between the real inner self who is interested in the ideals. This is distinct from the outer instrument or body and the personality that has grown up between the two, on account of the thought, "I am this."

Gaze at the hand; look at it intently as mere dissociated form, until you realize that it is not yourself. Apply the same thought to other parts of the body and to the body as a whole, also to the collection of emotional and mental habits commonly called the mind. Realize that your self lies deeper than any of these, that even as knower and known or subject and object can never be the same, you are not these things. Ask yourself whether in dealing with other people you have considered them as persons or as the real self. In this contemplation you will find Chapter XI of my book *Concentration* a great help (Wheaton: Theosophical Publishing House, 1981).

Resolve that at some future time you will give yourself in complete devotion to the inner self, and that during the coming day you will at least try to deal with events in full loyalty to it.

• EXERCISE 2—SECOND WEEK

Each morning think over the things which may probably occur during the day to throw you off

19

your balance of serene judgment, unfailing kindness, and calm decision. Picture their concrete occurrence in vivid imagination, and see yourself as passing through them without disturbance, but as the self within would wish. Then, during the day, occasionally recall this meditation and try to act in accord with it.

The exercises that are given in this course are not intended to be practiced for a long time so that they become monotonous, but for the week or two in which they are taken up they should be done with really earnest concentration. They will then permanently affect the character to a marked degree, and as a result of that, will bring students to a new platform, or to a higher rung of the ladder of progress, from which they will be well able to see what to do next.

II
Building Character

3

PREPARING THE GROUND

Now you must prepare the ground on which your building of character is to be raised, and for this our previous analysis of the two aspects of human nature will be particularly helpful. First, consider the personal aspect, made up of the body with its characteristics and a collection of habitual desires and thoughts developed mainly for your satisfaction throughout life. What is this personal self to you but an opinion of yourself? You have formed this opinion by contact with the world, looking, as it were, in the mirror of life, listening to the opinions of others about you, noticing their treatment of you, finding out your own abilities and disabilities, considering your appearance as compared with that of other people.

Behind that personality is the real self, capable of thinking, loving, willing, and expanding his consciousness to illimitable perfection. When the real self begins to show in the life of the personal self, character appears; as the self increases in power, character develops more and more; but you have to consider in the beginning the condition of your personal self, for this forms the ground on which your building is to be raised.

There are three characteristics of all forms in the material world: they are composed of matter, and thus have the quality of stability; they contain force in latent or active form, and have thus the quality of energy; they are subject to some law which limits their mass and motion and gives them shape and size and other qualities of form. These three qualities—stability, energy, and lawfulness—are to be found in the atom itself and in the most perfectly organized form on earth, the human body—of which you possess one specimen—as well as in all things between the two.

You will see that your personal self has attained all three of the qualities in abundant measure; if it has not, you are not likely to take active interest in the subject matter of this book. Stability you should have developed thousands of years ago in earlier bodies that loved to lie idly in the shade of palm or banyan when the day's work was done, when you learned to love the things that are, and deeply disliked all changes and inconveniences of the effort of adaptation that they brought. Later energy began to increase until excitement and adventure became the very spice of life. Later still you realized that you were part of a world of law and order and did not live simply for your own enjoyment of ease and excitement. You found that there were rules for eating and drinking, sleeping and waking, activity and rest, intercourse and solitude—in fact, that life was subject to laws, and the greatest pleasure was to be found in obedience to the natural laws of life. Then you became a virtuous member of civilized society, harmonizing your life with that of the cosmos around you.

Here is the danger now. You have so purified the personality that it is able to yield to the inner self because it has become subject to law. But before you begin the work of building character, make sure that you have not lost the virtues that formed the backbone of the vices of laziness and excitability—stability and energy. There is little use in being what is commonly called a good man, one obedient to the laws of health and social and individual morality, unless you have preserved the stability and energy of the earlier stages of growth. Feeble goodness is a poor thing at best, and goodness purchased at the cost of strength and energy is a delusion and a snare. There is much truth in the old proverb, "the greater the sinner, the greater the saint," for the sinner has often stability and energy that in the days of repentance will be used to great purpose in obedience to the laws of life. Purification of the personal self is not to be done by suppression of positive powers but by their development to greater heights, in obedience to the healthy laws of individual and social life.

Consider now the inner self working in the purified and obedient personality. There are some things in us that can be but dimly seen because of the glare of daily life. The sky is studded with stars by day as well as by night, but their points of light cannot be seen in the glare of daylight unless one looks up at them from the depths of a deep well or mine which excludes a great quantity of light. So in the human soul there is a spiritual light, unknown in the glare of daily life but visible to the mind's eye in the depths of meditation, when the activities of daily life and the emotions and thoughts connected with them are for the moment still.

No man acts from his judgment ultimately; all act from impulse or emotion or intuition—from the impulse of the body and mind, the emotions awakened by desire, or those fine intuitions giving both information and command. Intuitions can make themselves heard only when the personality

26

is silent, except, as the character develops, they now and then speak in the mind with a clear, bodiless voice.

This that we call intuition is a faculty in the spiritual depths of the soul, whereby information comes without sensation or judgment, and direction is given to life. But it is only valuable to one who has predetermined nothing and will accept with joy and perfect willingness any message or command from that inner source. It is small and quiet now because we are not far evolved. In time intuition will grow and flood the whole nature, so that the thinking mind will fall into second place as its humble servant in the human economy—just as the little seed of judgment in the animal, hidden amid a mass of natural impulses and desires, develops into the ruler in the human mind, coordinating and controlling impulse and desire. This intuition will come in different forms, to all types of persons of character, by their sinking occasionally into the well of meditation until they see the star-studded vault above.

• EXERCISE 3—THIRD WEEK

Taking care that there is no strain in the body which would produce a frown, a stiffness of the neck, or anything of the kind, sit with the eyes

27

closed and make a mental picture of your body. Then think of your feelings and thoughts about the things of your world, so as to form a more complete mental image of your own personality. Gradually drop the physical body out of your thought and keep your attention upon the emotional and mental part of your personality. Then drop the emotions and simply look at your thoughts. Finally calm down those thoughts and quietly look, as it were, into the vacant place, with hopeful expectancy of some glimmering of what is within. When it comes, this glimmering will bring you joy and irradiation of the mind. Do not try to grasp it—that cannot be done—but keep the mind open and turned to the vacancy until thoughts fall away, which they will do very soon. In order to receive intuitions, the mind must be free from desire for a particular result—or indeed for any result at all—and from prejudice, willing to receive anything that comes.

Equally important is the development of a permanent mood during the day. The flow of your thought with reference to every object that you meet in the course of daily life depends upon your mood. This has been carefully explained in the second chapter of my book, *Concentration*. Examine the thoughts and feelings that pass through your mind in a single day, or even in a single hour, and you will probably find that your personality is extremely discrete and incoherent. The mind is like a river carrying on its surface innumerable bits of wreckage of your many past plans and schemes and experiences—odds and ends picked up from the banks, floating for awhile and then sinking to the bottom or drifting out of the stream onto the banks again. All these odds and ends must be gathered together into the net of a permanent mood. Put in another way, the mind is like a pot of boiling water, bubbling and breaking into a thousand trifling emotions and thoughts in the course of an hour.

For the development of character you require a mind steadily controlled by a permanent mood, so that every incoming and uprising thought and emotion may be polarized to that. Just as an architect interested in his profession, passing through the streets of a city, notices the detail of every structure that he sees, because of his prevailing habit of thought about such things; just as a new mother notices babies wherever she goes; just as a new motorcyclist sees the make and condition of every other machine that passes him, so must you see during the practice of this course the significance of every thing and event that occurs to you in the light of its effect on the building of character. This results from the prevailing mood which you will set up at this stage of the work.

• Exercise 4—Fourth Week

Review the probable events of the coming day and, as you look at each in turn, consider what its effect will be upon your character—how it will affect your qualities of courage, of truth and of love. Resolve that each event shall be used for the building of your character, that is, for the development of these three qualities.

4

FOUNDATIONS OF COURAGE

If you have decided to take a distinct step in the development of your own character, to raise it from its present platform to another distinctly higher, you must first realize that the work you have set yourself is one of definite building, as precise and orderly as that of building a house. In building a house you would have to proceed deliberately, collecting and shaping your various materials and building them carefully and systematically into a definite plan. At the outset you would have to consider three main portions of the building, which are the essential parts of almost every building in the world—the foundations, the walls, and the roof.

There is one quality which lies at the root of all successful and permanent development of character, and that is courage. This should form the foundation of your building of character. You must realize what courage is, not so much in the abstract or in the deeds of distant heroes, but in your own life, whatever it may be. There is scarcely one other quality among all those that make up human character which does not involve this quality of courage. It is challenged when a little child tells her first lie when cornered by parents or teachers, under the influence of fear. The young lawyer admits his first doubtful evidence under the fear of loss of reputation or success and, behind that, poverty and insecurity of life for himself and family. The merchant first falls from honesty from the same cause.

In schools all over the world for a long time children have been driven to study under the rule of fear, whether from harsh words, ridicule, or failure to pass examinations and consequent failure in life. The result has been such an undermining of character that the average citizen can be relied upon not to support his convictions with courage but to barter them for comfort and security on the one hand or fame and glory on the other. In popular electioneering, how common is the appeal to personal and partisan advantage; how seldom is there an exhortation to hold fast to those things that are best, no matter what the personal sacrifice may be.

Fear is a retrograde emotion; it not only undermines character, as has been said above, but stops probably more than ninety percent of the original and progressive work which we are capable of doing, and throws us back constantly upon old methods of work, old social customs, and old religious bondages.

You have only to examine your own life to find to what a large extent you are leaning upon others—a practice which is fatal to the development of great strength of character. You may have beauty of character if your emotions are kind and good, but that is not sufficient for the making of a man or woman, and it is extremely doubtful how such qualities would stand the pressure of really trying circumstances. Tolstoy has pointed out in his book *My Religion* how grateful people are in their weakness to others upon whom they are permitted to lean, especially in matters of religion, which deals with the deeper problems and ultimate ends of life. Because of this weakness, people will cling desperately to illogical beliefs which are shared by many others, and if these are assailed, will fight with the fury of an animal for the props which are sustaining their miserable life.

All that sort of thing must go once and for all if you have determined to build your own character. While you are laying your foundation of courage, you will probably have to strike away a great many props and work hard to replace them by conscientious principles of your own.

It is not for yourself alone that the work is necessary. Every step forward in the progress of society was begun by a man of character who had the courage to face social and religious tyranny. We have already seen what part courage played in the discovery of inventions and the development of science and philosophy. Indeed, if we enjoy today any of the blessings of liberty, it is because there have been brave and wise men who fought with tongue, pen, and sword against selfishness and greed, in order that people might be free from slavery, be permitted to live on land and cultivate it, to carry on manufacturing and trade, to travel about, to follow their chosen religion, and to enjoy the fruits of their labor without molestation and deprivation. In public and private life, in large affairs and in small, courage is the foundation of success. It may be for this reason that in the *Bhagavad Gita*, Shri Krishna, in giving to Arjuna a list of qualities that make for human progress towards divinity, places courage first of all.

There are, then several practical things that you must do. First of all, you must work under difficulties, for they can aid you. It is not necessary to make difficulties, for everyone receives a reasonable number of them without that. It would be unwise to rush into great difficulties, just as it would be foolish to start physical exercises with dumbbells weighing ten pounds each. There is a certain moderation in which growth can best be obtained. Next, try to realize that the things that are considered pleasant are as much trials for the character as those from which we shrink. Riches are as dangerous as poverty, and health is even more of a test than disease. As the world is a school for the development of character, each of these things must be valued for that purpose, without undue regard to what is pleasant and disagreeable. Then you must have faith in life. There are no barriers to success but those that exist within yourself.

• EXERCISE 5—FIFTH AND SIXTH WEEKS

Sit down quietly each morning and dwell upon the quality of courage. Think of anything that might occur during the coming day that would be disagreeable to you, that you would shrink from on account of shyness, fear of ridicule, laziness, or mistrust of your own powers. Picture the incident very clearly. Then decide calmly what you really ought to do in the matter, putting aside all questions of fear. Complete the picture by imagining yourself in it as actually doing the thing upon which you have decided. When the incident does crop up, try to act as you have decided, but do not waste your energy in vain regrets if you happen to fail. Just begin again.

• EXERCISE 6—FIFTH AND SIXTH WEEKS

Whenever you have commanded your body to do anything, see that it does that thing unless you have a good reason to change your purpose. If, for example, you have fixed a time for rising on any day, see that no laziness or sluggishness is permitted to delay you and do not break your rule for a reason less deliberate than that which made it. If you have decided to purchase some trifling thing while in town, and on your return you find that you have carelessly overlooked the matter, make your body go back and get the thing accepting no excuse or rebellion.

• EXERCISE 7—SIXTH AND SEVENTH WEEKS

Everyday do something, however trifling, that is contrary to your regular habits—preferably something useful, of course. If you are addicted to novels, do some hard study; if you are very fond of your food, leave out a meal, or try dry bread and water; if you are a feverish worker, put in a lazy time.

The whole purpose of these exercises is to develop courage and self-control and bring your will into activity. Good habits are very valuable because they leave energy for higher things, but to allow them entire control of life is to weaken the foundation of your building.

5

THE SUPPORT OF
TRUTHFULNESS

We come now to the second essential part of your building—the walls which stand upon the foundations and support the roof. There are two very important features of the walls of a building that is to be both tall and safe—they must be absolutely straight and true, and their material must be of good quality without serious flaws. The walls of skyscrapers may be only a few inches in thickness in many places. Thick walls of brick of such a height would be destroyed by their own weight, for the upper part of the wall pressing upon the bricks below would crumble them to powder. But the fine steel ribs of those great buildings, erected with perfect accuracy in the perpendicular, are safe for far more than the load that is put upon them. In all such building, it is quality that is important, not quantity.

What in character corresponds to these walls? It is the virtue of truth. If your building of character is to rise high and strong, its walls must be upright and steady with perfect truth. Great quantities of knowledge are not necessary, but what there is should be accurate. Do not be eager for a great quantity of knowledge or achievement, but be anxious about the quality. You must make your ideas clear-cut and decided, and see that they are not vitiated by personal desires. Thus you will build your character according to the gravity of the spiritual law of truth.

For success in this work, you must desire truth above everything else and be willing to know things exactly as they are, not colored by your desire that they should be different. In this wishing, as is explained in *Concentration*, is a cause of great weakness. You must try to find out exactly where you stand with respect to different qualities as compared with other people, decide what you want next, and then use your will to put that decision into effect. In this examination you may find that your walls are not true, that you have in this or that small matter distorted or weakened them by dishonesty or hypocrisy or some other such thing, or that you have built into them some rotten material on account of self-deception, which has raised them too high.

It is for you now, with perfect indifference to pleasure or pain, to pull down that rotten and bad work and begin on a foundation of courage. You must not wish that anything should be in the least different from what it is, but be anxious to know things exactly as they are, without the least regard for your own comfort or self-satisfaction.

If you build without this fundamental honesty, your walls can never be high and strong. Every faulty brick that you put in, every piece of careless workmanship, will endanger the entire structure and surely bring you much trial and struggle at some future time. Put in familiar language, every piece of deception, whether self-deception or deception of others, will lead to lie after lie in thought, word, and action, until the whole structure comes crashing to the ground.

The work of self-examination is extremely difficult, for it is quite possible that you may belong to one of those two unfortunate classes of people—those who habitually overrate their own powers and those who habitually underrate them. If you belong to the former class, you will put the best construction upon your thoughts and acts, and if to the latter you will put the worst. There is only one way out of the difficulty: during the time of judgment you must get yourself into a condition of what is called *vairagya* among the Hindu yogis.

The word means detachment, that the mind in its judgment shall not be discolored or agitated by personal desires arising from its attachment to pleasures or fear of pains. During self-examination you must put all wishes aside and make your calm judgment as upon a person in whom you take no interest whatever.

After this, a general habit of honesty towards yourself may be set up. Many people have a tendency to overvalue their own preferences or undervalue those of others, for their own self-satisfaction. Thus the average man thinks his own religion is better than other people's, often with no shadow of reason for his opinion. The bookworm despises athletics, and the athlete despises the bookworm. The young lover thinks his sweetheart the most delightful being on earth and the young mother that her baby is the most wonderful. "It would not do," said Mr. A., "for every one to think alike, for if they did, they would all have wanted to marry my wife." "Quite so," returned Mr. B., "and if they had thought as I do, no one would have married her." Some people pride themselves on being professionals, others on being businessmen, others on their position in labor. But exaggerating one's importance does not increase happiness in the long run.

There is another form of allegiance to truth in

the mode of doing work. There is only one kind of work that will do, and that is what is called honest work, which is work with an eye to quality rather than to quantity. Every time that you do a piece of work better than you have done it before, as for example a piece of writing, you have trained hand, nerve, eye, and brain, and developed some additional power of self-control and will. But if you did the work a thousand times in the same old style with no effort at improvement, you would have gained nothing but a faculty produced by habit. Faculty is not a thing of great value to the soul, though it has its convenience in the world. It may even lead one astray, as in the case in which facility of words tempts one to speak too much without sufficient thought.

Criticism by others can also be used as a great help to self-training. Instead of receiving it with annoyance and irritability because perhaps it obstructs your work in the outer world, it is worthwhile to examine criticism for the germ of truth that it nearly always contains.

Then comes the question of truth in relation to others. Deception not only corrupts one's own character but also undermines society. If a person is once deceived, he tends to look for deception elsewhere. Customers are cheated in a store; children lie to their parents; businessmen cheat on their income taxes; public officials dip into public funds; nations covertly arm against one another. Mistrust and suspicion arise, and social progress is shattered. All social progress depends upon the development of social consciousness and its attendant conscience, and this in turn upon mutual trust.

Anyone who proceeds to corrupt society by untruth is sure to receive his reward of being mistrusted and deceived. There are few or no cases in which deception is *permissible*. I know the case of a hospital patient to whom the nurses lied in order to assuage his delirium. After a little time he found out that their words were not true and began to regard them as sinister, with the result that there was great struggle and difficulty and a serious relapse. Too often patients misunderstand their doctors because they believe that the latter are in the habit of concealing the truth. There are many kind people who would sacrifice truth to kindness, but undoubtedly that policy leads to greater sorrow on the whole and in the long run.

In relation to the world around us, another form of allegiance to truth is an open mind and a willingness to see greatness anywhere, not only in those things and persons which have been labeled great by society and religious bodies. We never know where the next thing will rise that is going to revolutionize the world for good. No one in the fifteenth century could have expected that letters of the alphabet placed on a movable base would revolutionize the world. Yet Gutenberg and other printers, using an idea already developed in China and Korea, produced presses that eventually brought the printed page to millions and led to literacy for common people throughout the world. Great things often arise in the world from the most obscure and unexpected places, through people of sterling character, of strong will and insight and love for their fellows in the little world that happens to be theirs.

● EXERCISE 8—EIGHTH WEEK

Set aside fifteen minutes each evening to examine selected portions of the day's actions and conversations. Go over them again in thought, and judge the extent to which they were intended to deceive oneself or others. Resolve that such injurious untruth shall cease, and observe that silence is better than untruthful or injurious speech.

● EXERCISE 9—EIGHTH AND NINTH WEEKS

Take up some small piece of artistic work, such as a few bars of music or a small sketch, or write a few lines—*better* than you have ever done it before. Do this each day.

44

6
THE PROTECTION OF LOVE

The chief purpose of the roof of a building is to protect those who are within from rain and snow and from the too great heat of the sun. It is therefore but natural that we should take the roof as the symbol of the quality of love, which—understood in a general way and apart from all sentimentality—means unselfish motive. It is constantly becoming more widely realized that humanity is one, indeed that those qualities that we regard as distinctively human are those which are opposed to struggle and competition. Many realize now that cooperation is the law of human progress and that a benefit to any man reacts upon the whole of humanity. What has been called the solidarity of humanity is becoming an established fact in social science. It seems obvious that it is only selfishness, based upon ignorance, which prevents mankind from reaching immediately a social and economic millenium.

When you begin the work of roofing in your building, first of all you have to see that your motives are not selfish, that is to say that they do not direct you to purposes which are definitely injurious to others or tending towards their degradation. If you aim, for example, to increase your wealth—money and property, which resolve themselves into power over the lives and fortunes of others less successful or more unfortunate than yourself—it can only be on the ground that it is for the purpose of general benefit. You must also remember that everyone requires liberty for the development of his powers, so that in no case is the pursuit of power permissible to any great extent. It is not by exerting power over others that we can help them most, but by causing them to awaken their own powers.

Desire to see other people happy and well provided with the things that they need leads to emotions of love. Expressions of love can vary to an enormous extent, from the great compassion of a mother for her helpless little child, through the friendship of comrades, to the reverence and devotion that people pay to God. In all these cases one feels unity of interest so strongly that the material barriers of self seem to be transcended, and the hidden unity, which is perceived by spiritual intuition, impresses itself (generally quite unconsciously) upon the emotional nature. I know of a case of this sense of unity becoming for a moment so powerful that one person observing a fly settle on the nose of another tried to knock it off his own.

Those who have had first glimpses of their existence on earth in previous lives often experience a curious realization of the self as independent of any particular form. I know one case of a man who suddenly saw a vision of himself in the form of an Indian woman who lived long ago. The sensation was described as recognizing himself in a mirror. When this man realized that this woman was himself, he had exactly the same sensation that he knew himself as when he looked into a mirror and saw the reflection of his present body. He no longer identified himself with that body.

Unselfish emotion, therefore, does not mean martyrdom for the self. It means that the personal consciousness is becoming more exalted, so that it can expand itself in the life of others instead of in the multiplicity of material things to be used for very temporary enjoyment. This means an accession of life and happiness, for while material pleasures quickly die away, there is no limit to the spiritual happiness that comes from love, from progressive realization of truth, and from creative work.

Every religious teacher, coming among a people

torn by ignorance and strife, has affirmed this law: the life of kindness and helpfulness is the only one that can lead to lasting happiness. They have all worked to spread peace among men so as to bring about a unity of the people. The lives of Christ and Mohammed are full of this effort and teaching. The Lord Buddha taught that hatred ceaseth not by hatred at any time, but ceaseth only by love. Shri Krishna, speaking in the *Bhagavad Gita* as the Divine Lord, explained that there is no reason why he should descend into the world and work unceasingly, for there is no duty that he is bound to do and no thing that he desires. But if he did not perform action, others following him would cease from action, and others in ever descending series would follow their example, and the social order would fall into ruin. Immediately upon that explanation, he exhorted Arjuna to work without personal desire, as other great men had worked before him, desiring only the unity of the people. Here is the implication that the Divine Lord loved the human race and therefore moved to preserve it from ruin.

The work of building character at this stage consists, first of all, in examining your motives and putting them under the law of love. Second, the emotions have to be trained, and any akin to anger or hatred or cruel pride or selfish fear must be converted into friendliness or benevolence or reverence, so that emotions may work no injury in the outer world to another person or in the mind to yourself. How this may be done in detail will be seen in the chapter on the emotions. Here only one thing needs to be said. There is a little key, one turn of which may convert any unkind or unloving emotion into one of kindness, for the strengthening of yourself and the improvement of your relationships. The turning of that key requires a simple act of will in controlling your thought. You must stop thinking of yourself and think instead of the consciousness and happiness of the person who has awakened the undesirable emotion in you.

If, for example, you suddenly have a feeling of proud contempt for another who may be more degraded than yourself, you may, by ceasing to contemplate your own superiority with self-satisfaction, transfer your center of consciousness to the other's mind. You may realize in some measure what he is thinking and feeling, and your contempt will turn to compassion and a desire to lift him up. If your friend, in a moment of anger, said something that wounded your feelings, you turn that little key and see how for the moment the world appears to her. You may sympathize with some trouble that has disturbed her mind and respond with perfect friendliness instead of anger. If your boss is particularly short with you one morning, instead of going away in fear and self-pity, you will realize that he has been annoyed by some incident that perhaps had nothing at all to do with you. You will perhaps realize the dificulty of his position of responsibility, and your own emotion will be converted into admiration for one who bears great responsibilities with comparatively little loss of balance. In any case you have something to learn from anyone who can frighten you and therefore some cause for gratitude towards him.

• EXERCISE 10—TENTH WEEK

Be on the lookout for occasions on which you feel any form or degree of (a) unkind pride, (b) hatred, or (c) fear. Deliberately pause when the occasion comes, stop thinking of your own feelings, and think of the feelings and thought of the person who has offended you. Observe the sudden change in yourself.

• EXERCISE 11—ELEVENTH WEEK

Give some time to the study of your motives for various actions.

7
THE OUTER SELF

Living alone within the building that you have erected, you may have developed great qualities of courage, truth, and affection. Yet your house may appear to the visitor somewhat stern and forbidding in aspect. You know that it is attractive within, but, if the exterior is left plain and square without any ornaments, it is only to be expected that others will not recognize that attractiveness within, and you will be to some extent shut out from that relationship that ought to be pleasant and profitable, both to you and to them.

We have therefore to consider at this point the verandahs and pleasant entrances to your house, by means of which it may be tempered to the climate and made agreeable to all who pass by. Your verandah might be made like one in Victorian India, where every passing traveler could tether his horse, find sweet water for his use, and lie down for refreshment in the heat of the day or for restful sleep at night.

The exterior of your life, that is to say, must be rendered pleasant and inviting, with whatever beauty of form, grace, manners, and bearing you may find to be appropriate in your place and time. However retiring you may be by disposition, you will in this way do much good to others and gain still more for yourself. Most people, indeed, will never really know you but will only enter upon the verandah of your life and character, where that which is within may overflow in constant cheerfulness and good humor. Thus you present those prepossessing qualities which facilitate success and progress in friendship, and indeed in all the outward affairs of life.

Without such outward graces, you may have great qualities and still be an ungainly member of society. This will react in two ways, as living alone nearly always does. It may develop great strength in particular directions but leave great weaknesses in the character as companions to these great virtues, and it may leave a person eccentric, awkward, and disagreeable in social relationship. On the other hand, those who spend time in the midst of the society of their fellows, thinking but little about self-preparation for the future but always trying to make themselves agreeable, develop an all-round character and are very pleasant as social companions, though possessed of no great strength of character and showing no great defects.

These two types of people consciously or unconsciously obey the two paradoxical behests of religion everywhere—that a man should make great efforts to improve himself, and that he should grow as the flower grows: "Consider the lilies of the field, how they grow; they toil not, neither do they spin: and yet I say unto you, that even Solomon in all his glory was not arrayed like one of these." There will always be some people who are lilies of the field, fitting perfectly into their social environment, gifted with ease of manner and expression, and feeling no strain upon life because there is no great difference between the inner and the outer person, between ideals and conduct. These people are bright, dependable, likable, useful in an established order. But they generally have no great originality and feel no call to dispute established customs or to decide anything anew. They live mainly on the verandah, and it is well for them if they have the company of the great and the good, if they work with them, live with them, play with them, and "grow as the flower grows, opening its heart to the sun."

Only one warning is necessary at the close of this subject—to avoid the methods of a certain class of people who have hidden purposes of self-satisfaction and pride within and cultivate society and friends for their own fame or selfish gain. These are not lilies of the field but dangerous weeds, and for the time being they are not in a state of healthy human growth. True human progress requires that when we associate with others we shall do so primarily for their benefit and with a view to the fulfillment of their needs, not for the advancement of our own. Even when you help another, it is not important that you are the helper but that he is being helped.

8
THE PLACE OF PLAY

In the midst of this strenuous work, you need health and the benefits of a well-balanced life, suppleness, and beauty of character and form. In this physical world your work cannot be highly successful, except in a narrow way, unless time is reserved for play, which is called recreation by those who do not realize that the whole of life is but the play of God. Hence the need of a garden around your house, where you can at odd times lie about and dream, run about and play.

The characteristics of play are two. It gives us the pleasure of using our powers and enjoying healthy sensations, and it stops short of the point when fatigue becomes uncomfortable. The delight of riding a bicycle, for example, gives us a feeling of added power, which comes from the smooth and swift gliding motion, the exhilarating sensation of air rushing past and objects flitting by, and the enhanced glow of life in the body on account of the healthy, vigorous exercise. If we are tempted to go a long distance, we may become very tired on the return journey; then all pleasure disappears and we only wish that we were back at home. It is no longer play; it is drudgery, because we have to continue making efforts beyond the point of healthy tiredness.

Walking, running, jumping, skipping, swimming, singing, and various kinds of ball games such as football, tennis, and golf, are all favorite forms of play. They give us the pleasure of using physical power and skill and create a healthy physical glow, unless they are overdone. It is a good rule in play as in eating, to stop before you are fully satisfied.

All creatures that are not by nature sluggish and are not overworked or underfed share with humans this delight in play, which is so necessary for the health of the body. We see young lambs and calves frisking about in the fields and hear the birds enjoying themselves with song. Those who are familiar with wild monkeys will have noticed what delight they take in chasing one another among the trees and gamboling together on the ground, pulling one another's tails and jumping and leaping over one another's heads. The life of animals is generally so well arranged that work and recreation are the same for them, and there is no hurry or strain. Each detail of both work and play is interesting because of its complete relation to life.

However, deliberate play is necessary for us, especially for those who are engaged in sedentary work, which generally tires the eyes and nerves and leaves the muscles weak and flabby. Physical exercises that can be done in the home are necessary also for toning up the system of the sedentary worker. A selection of these can be found in many books on the subject.

The brain also requires recreation, especially when it is tired owing to ill-balanced living. Under these circumstances, relief may be obtained by reading stories and good novels with light emotional interest of love, adventure, or mystery, and by playing indoor games such as chess. Allied to these are the many hobbies which give light and healthy scope for the exercise of art and skill. But we should set limits to our indoor recreation, so as not to waste time that ought to be spent in study, work, or healthy outdoor recreation, or in other duties. We must not waste precious hours in games of chance that create unhealthy excitement.

It is important that play should be play and should not be spoiled by being taken too seriously or being tainted with ambition. An instance of this is the feeling that music in the home is generally so much inferior to professional music that it loses its attraction. But, really, the music and singing of those we love at home, though it may be very far from perfect, is far more restful and pleasant than that which our critical faculty so much approves in the concert hall or on television or the radio. Baseball is another example. As long as children play with a bat and ball on any bit of ground that is available, there will be pleasure. But the joy often goes when they become ambitious and spend their energy in worrying about perfection of the kind prescribed by the professionals who make a work of the game.

9
HONEST WORK

There is one thing more which is absolutely necessary before your house can be regarded as complete, and that is the orchard. It symbolizes that part of your life which is productive to the outer world. Nothing lives by itself, and you must give as well as take, producing fruit of hand or brain for yourself and others. The basis of your life in the outer world will therefore be a definite occupation, which must be beneficial, not useless or in any degree harmful.

Your work may be directly productive or distributive or protective. If it belongs to the first class, it must be beneficial in the production of something useful, beautiful, amusing, instructive, or inspiring, and your occupation may then be that of farmer, laborer or supervisor, factory worker, artisan, domestic worker or manager, artist, author, or something of the kind. If it is in the second class, you may be in sales, advertising, or transportation; merchant, or trader; or in the third, policeman, lawyer, magistrate, or legislator.

Since civilization is a state of human society organized for the humane production and just distribution of true wealth—including spiritual, moral, mental, emotional, and physical riches—benefit can be secured only by what contributes to the progress of these things. You should be careful in the first place to produce articles of lasting value to the public, those that appeal to a good motive for possession, and cultivate a taste for high quality, so as to raise the standard of living for the people for whom they are intended. In the second case, you should bring the goods so produced within the reach of those who need them, and distribution is to be for the benefit of the public. All such practices as that of cornering and profiteering are a crime against civilization and a means of degradation of character for those who do such things.

We may take one or two examples. If you own a shop, it is your business to see that it is a real convenience to the people in your neighborhood, that you provide the kind of things that will be most serviceable to them, so that you can feel that whenever a customer leaves your shop she will not regret having bought the article that you sold her. You must therefore make yourself a judge of the honest merits of the things you sell, mark your prices with a fair proportion of profit, and avoid those goods which you know to be produced by workers who are forced to work too hard, under bad conditions, and for less than a reasonable living wage. In that way you will be doing good to your neighborhood, and you will get a reputation for honesty. People will be glad to trade with you and thankful that you have helped them to understand that it is better and cheaper occasionally to buy good things that are handsome and durable than to buy cheap and showy rubbish more frequently.

If you are a lawyer, you will desire only that the judge before whom you present your case shall know to the full the facts of the case and the truth as you know it, and in this way you will get a reputation for honesty, so that only those who feel that they are thoroughly in the right will dare to come to you. In this way you will help the magistrate or judge, the honest litigant, and the sacred cause of justice. If you become a teacher or a scientist, you will be a devotee of truth, for it is no business of yours to become an advocate for any particular policy, to suppress the facts that do not suit that policy and lay undue emphasis upon those that do, but only to discover and disseminate the truth.

Whenever you practice or prepare for your definite occupation, you must have in view a definite ideal to which you aspire and a definite virtue with which you work. These three, occupation, ideal and virtue, must always be kept together. For example, as a magistrate or lawyer, your ideal may be justice and your virtue truth; as a sales person, your ideal may be prosperity and your virtue honesty; as a clerk or typist, your ideal may be perfect quality or workmanship and your virtue diligence or perseverance; as a domestic worker your ideal may be peace and your virtue considerateness.

In each case you must select the ideal and the virtue for yourself for a fixed period, a month or a year, and then change it if you so desire. In this way you learn to live the life of a spiritual person in the midst of the world's activity, which may be harder and more full of falls, but is far more worthwhile than the spiritual life lived in seclusion, away from the temptations of daily life.

Some people will meet you on the verandah, others in the gardens, others in the orchard, and your social relationships will differ in the three cases. It is well to realize that people who can work together harmoniously cannot always play together. You need not be agitated by the troubles of social inequality, but realize that in a perfect system each has his own orbit. Jupiter may be farther than Venus from the sun but this detracts nothing from his size and power.

10
THREE SOUL QUALITIES

If you have practiced to any extent the course so far described, you will have discovered that the three qualities of courage, truth, and love have not been selected at random but are fundamental to character. Under those three every other quality that you can mention comes in as subordinate. A close inspecton of character will show that these are the three fundamental virtues, or means of progress towards human perfection. They end, so far as we are able to see, in three things which are so much part of the soul itself that no human being is born without an instinctive desire for them: namely, freedom, realization of the truth about things, and a full sense of the unity of life.

Unity of life is the goal as it appears to those who are affectionate and devotional; realization of the fullness of life to those who are attached to knowledge and truth; and freedom to those of courage and will. Yet when any one of these is considered in any degree of perfection, it will be seen that it includes the other two. Though in a given human character one of the three qualities may be stronger than the other two, none can ever be absent. They are a trinity in unity, inseparable.

It is inevitable, though not altogether desirable, that one of these should predominate in your character, and even that you should concentrate upon it more than upon the others. The undesirable element comes in directly when you have to deal with other persons—on the verandah, in the garden and the orchards. This can be thought out in detail. One or two hints will suffice here.

Kindness and love that limit the freedom of the loved one do much to destroy gratitude and even embitter the gift. Rash plunges at freedom through acts of courage dictated by the will, lacking in judgment and affection, produce much trouble in the world. And indirectly all such forms of trouble arising from our unbalanced characters react upon the circumstances of our own life, as will be seen more clearly in a later chapter. Still, the unbalance cannot be avoided and need not be grieved over. No one can pay strong and clear attention to more than one thing at a time, though a clear vision of the fundamental relation among the three will produce the effect of bringing up the other two, at least in the penumbra of your vision, while your attention is focused on one.

It is interesting to find confirmation of this view in the *Bhagavad Gita.* Shri Krishna, after telling Arjuna that the greatest gift that a man can make is the one that is accompanied by knowledge, then tells him that he can realize this truth, not by study alone, but by three things—reverence, enquiry, and service. That is to say, nothing can be truly known by thinking about it. It can be truly known only by the soul that gives the best of thought, the best of emotion, and the best of action in the search. It is these three things taken together that constitute human life, and in each person they exist in different degrees and proportions.

To sum up the above facts, you will find that religious persons seek unity through love, realization through truth, and freedom through courage, and these three perfections of the soul correspond with the omnipresence, the omniscience, and the omnipotence of the Divine Being.

As the three ends of the virtues of courage, truth, and love are perfect qualities of the soul, in setting our faces towards them and walking with a will, we are really striving to be our full and true selves. It is due to lack of self-realization that we are caught in all the meshes of confusion in the outer world. No one is bad, no one lacks the three qualities, but people forget who they are and cease to be themselves, ever and again. We live intermittently, instead of constantly, as will be more clearly shown in the chapter on the three fundamental vices.

- EXERCISE 12—TWELFTH WEEK

Study the character which moves your actions during the day. Observe the elements of courage, truth, and love; and try to discover how far you are moved by fondness for creative work, eagerness for useful knowledge, and love for your fellow beings.

III

Finding Your Type

11
YOUR GREATEST STRENGTH

At this stage of enquiry and practice, you need another piece of knowledge to guide your progress. Without it you may try to follow another man's path instead of your own—like a mango tree aspiring to be a coconut tree, or like a pine longing to be an oak. You must find out what kind of person you are and what is the greatest power in you. Is it love or understanding or will or the inspiration of beauty or religious devotion or scientific knowledge? Whatever it is, you must use this power, first to inspire and strengthen your weaker qualities, and then to lead them in full battle array into the field of life, with all its thought, feeling, and action.

People differ in the construction of character, and will do so to the end. The consciousness of each one of us is a growing, unfolding thing. That of a Shakespeare, an Einstein, a Tagore is a globe of glorious light compared with the feeble glow of the average person. It is brilliant and large and ever becoming more vivid and expansive. So grows the consciousness, until the human brain can no more contain it than the brain of a cow can carry the consciousness of a man. Then human experience will be at an end, and the divine (self-shining) life will begin.

Up to that very point, your leading quality and power will remain the guide and prompter of all the rest. That quality you must find, and you must use it. Never let it work alone—it needs the support of all the rest, though they take their very strength from its prompting. Through it, but with their aid, all your triumphs will be achieved, both in the inner world of your own thoughts and feelings and in the outer world of action and reaction. Your leading quality is for you the magic wand with which you can and will sooner or later command your world.

How is it to be found?

Test yourself and your life by careful introspection. You have done something—*why?* You have run for public office, written a book, promoted a trading company, started a shop, painted a picture, taken to athletics, bought a car—anything you like. *Why?* No common answer will do: "Oh, I felt the need of a change. I wanted something to do. I needed money for my family. I wanted to enlighten the public. I wanted better health." But *why?* And again *why*, to your trivial and superficial answer. What do you *want?*

Perhaps your fundamental need is to do things. You seek knowledge, not because you want knowledge but as it helps you to do what you want. You make friends—ultimately for the same reason. It is not knowledge and love you want first of all; it is the use of your will in action. You bring everything to its aid like a general studying the country, not because he is interested in it, but for the purposes of battle.

Perhaps your fundamental power is love, and you are full of sympathy for your fellows. You may seek knowledge and perform actions, but these subserve your sense of unity with other people and your insatiable desire for their happiness.

Perhaps you desire above all to understand life, and to this end you have to live a life of activity and mingle closely with your fellows. You will surely develop sympathy and the will to act, but through your fundamental hunger for knowledge of things as they really are.

Perhaps you are moved most of all by reverence for law that we call science, by reverence for love that we call religious devotion, or by reverence for beauty in all things and their relationships.

Question yourself once, twice, a hundred times, day after day, until you find what it is that most prompts your actions, trivial as well as great. Then apply that quality to the development of your weaker qualities, so that the whole character may become well balanced and free from the positive vice which always appears when one quality is strong and the others are weak.

For example, if you act from love, study wisdom and develop determination for the sake of love, so that it may not be foolish, injurious, or ineffective. If you act from desire for understanding, mingle lovingly with others, so that your judgment may not be warped by lack of sympathy and close contact, or by a limited point of view. If you act for the love of work, strive for the development of understanding and love, so that your work may not be purposeless or harmful. And in outer effects of your actions, seek to preserve reverence for law, love, and beauty.

With this idea in view, study carefully the next seven chapters, which are intended to help you find your leading power. Quite probably you will find that two of the seven mentioned are strongly marked, that sometimes one and sometimes the other takes command of your character.

One of the greatest benefits in discovering your own type will be that you can henceforth act with a

74

direct motive. Drifting will be at an end. When the eye is single, the mind will be full of light. If you want, for example, accurate knowledge, you will distinctly work with that desire. You will cultivate your other faculties (the will, devotion, sense of beauty, and the rest), so that they will do their best in their own way (through energy, intimacy of contact, responsiveness, and other powers) to help carry out the main purpose for which you directly live. Indirect motives producing action not true to your type have to be constantly pumped up, but direct motive provides a gushing well of soul energy.

• EXERCISE 13—THIRTEENTH WEEK

Question yourself as above indicated.

12
WILL POWER

We have now to consider more fully the leading qualities with which individuals are endowed. Each of these is related to an ideal or ultimate aim, and each has its own characteristic virtue.

We may take first the person of will, whose ideal is freedom. Justice is his virtue because he seeks to make others strong and free, and courage is his instrument of progress, because he is a person of decision and must often act without waiting to see clearly the reason why.

There has been much discussion about the nature of the will, and many attempts have been made to define its characteristics. It is sufficient for us to know that will is present in our own consciousness and to feel its working. It is as impossible to define will as it is to define consciousness, or anything else subjective. Subjective states cannot be defined in terms of objective things or their qualities or relationships. If will could be so defined, it would then be objective. By experience we know that we will, just as we know that we think and feel. Nor need we raise the question, What makes you will? It is sufficient to know that will is a power within us and that we can learn to apply it self-consciously, just as we can think self-consciously—or, rather, we can become self-conscious with regard to will.

It would be a mistake to assume that you use the will only on great occasions when you make a special decision. Its action is present in the slightest voluntary movement of your little finger. Will no more ceases than thought and feeling do; it is coextensive with life and consciousness.

Training of the will is twofold—as applied in your relation to yourself and to others. First, it means self-control in the three regions of your personal being—your physical body, your emotions, and your thoughts about things. Such self-control leads to a reflection of the ideal of freedom in the personality. As regards the physical body, you must train it into a condition of perfect constitutional fitness (not necessarily of great muscular strength, because that is a matter rather of quantity than of quality) and strive to make your environment fit in with the same purpose. As regards the emotions, self-control means the control of all of those that agitate you, such as fear and anger and the kind of pride that can be wounded. As regards the thinking mind, it means the abolition of prejudices which distort the mind and prevent its healthy action.

Without such self-control in all three parts of the personality, there can be no real personal freedom, for you will be constantly dragged this way and that by every trifling circumstance that has power to injure, agitate, and mislead you.

The second part of the training, which concerns your relation to others, requires that you win for them the same measure of freedom that you seek for yourself, that you help them in their circumstances and in their self-control. This means that you do not seek to prop them up in matters in which they are capable of helping themselves and so developing their own powers. You must be a reflection of the god who "helps them that help themselves," for any help that is purely external, that does not call out in any degree the soul powers of the one who is helped, is injurious.

Further, you must help others by putting power and opportunity in their hands. To cling to power and deprive others of it, under the guise of a desire to gain much power in order to help others, is one of the greatest dangers of this path. The pursuit of fame also makes for the bondage of others, for it is not desirable that one should fill other people's minds with oneself. In doing that we reproduce that viciously selfish characteristic of the modern novel which causes us to feel the greatest sympathy for the hero in his misfortunes but pass over carelessly the even greater misfortunes of subordinate characters.

The pursuit of freedom, for self and others, thus becomes very much a path of action, faith, and sacrifice. Because the intelligence is subordinate to the will, there will be many leaps in the dark, many efforts and actions of which the result cannot be seen. These call for the greatest courage and faith in principles whose working out cannot be clearly seen.

Those who follow this course do not have the satisfaction of seeing clearly that comes to those who are first thinkers and secondly actors. The wilful person does not even have those fitful flashes of satisfaction that come to one of devotional feeling and alternately raise him to ecstasy and lower him to depths of gloom. But later, the person of will has the satisfaction of feeling in himself that working of the will which brings its own ecstasy, just as deep philosophic thought or profound devotion can do. In each case the ecstasy is a conscious living in the soul.

The outward form of personal training is not unlike that described by the ancient Stoics, who put their happiness in the will, not in any outward thing. Their first aim was to decide which things were in their power and which were not, and, when they had so decided, to concern themselves (in thought, emotion, and action) only with the former. Thus the only thing the Stoic had to fear was himself, lest he fail rightly to use his powers upon those things which came within their scope. Just as we take care of our houses, land, and other possessions and protect them from decay, and just as we train our horses to keep them fit, so, the Stoic argues, should we treat this personality, the physical body, the emotions and the thinking mind, and train all these as healthy, useful, and happy servants of the will. There is nothing more in our power than our own personality; it is the one region from which God has withdrawn himself in order that we may be kings. Here indeed we should exercise our power, and exercise it rightly. An illustration of this is the story of the Stoic thrown into prison who refused to be agitated, and said to his captor: "You have taken possession of this body. It is now in your power, and you are responsible for what happens to it. It is not in my power and is therefore no concern of mine."

It is sometimes thought that self-assertion, arrogance, and a bullying disposition indicate will power. Nothing could be farther from the truth. Power is ease, and the will is the quietest thing in the world.

The scientific definition of power includes the conception of time. A man and a boy may both be able to lift a thousand bricks on to a wall, but if the man can do it in an hour and the boy requires two hours to complete the task, we say that the man has greater power. The greater his power, the greater will be the ease with which he does the work. So it is not the fussy or noisy or blustering person who shows will, but the one who calmly pursues his object without yielding, even when the means to success are not clearly in view. Will is preeminently self-determination—an innate predisposition not to be diverted by external things. The boaster, on the other hand, seeking the good opinion of the world, is very much the servant of circumstances.

The special virtue of the person of will is justice, which seeks to give to each the best opportunity for the development of his own powers, and hence for progress towards the ideal of freedom.

There are two great dangers for the will type, and it is well to be on guard against them. They are selfishness and thoughtlessness, which lead to a numerous band of lesser evils, not the least of which are cruelty and a disposition to dominate others.

There is a tendency for people on this line to push their purposes to success, sometimes at the sacrifice of truth and kindness when those qualities are weak and circumstances press for action. This defect has to be overcome by deliberately practicing acts of kindness and by maintaining truth under difficulties.

From this point onward you will have to frame your own exercises, as they depend on the discoveries you will now make about your own character. My book *The Seven Rays* (Wheaton: Theosophical Publishing House, 1984) contains additional information about the various types.

13
LOVE

People are realizing more and more the necessity for cooperation with one another and the benefits that arise from it. It is seen more clearly than ever before that co-operation does not mean the working together of those who think and feel alike, but rather of those who differ in ideals and character and in talents and ability, so that a perfect cosmos may be built of various materials and forms.

The whole work of what is called the law of evolution is really to convert chaos into cosmos by relating all things together more and more. Even defined as a progressive differentiation and integration, it is seen as the law of love, bringing all things together into a close organic relationship. To see this law and instinctively obey it is characteristic of this second type of people, who are wise in seeing and feeling the unity of all.

The unity of humanity does not depend upon a similarity of instincts; that would produce the unity of action that is seen in a flock of sheep. True unity rests upon a deeply rooted spiritual instinct which will not allow the one who possesses it to ignore the conscious life of others, however different from his own their ideals and methods of progress may be. Behind all the diversity, there is a unity of consciousness in the subjective world, just as behind all material objects there is a unity of fundamental substance. This unity appears in man as the spiritual instinct of sympathy, the power to feel with others, which is present wherever there is love of any degree or kind.

The second path of progress towards perfection and happiness is that which has unity as its ideal or end, sympathy with all living things as its virtue, and deep-seated love as its instrument of progress. If you belong to the type of people for whom this is the path, you will be a philanthropist of some kind, one of the followers of the way of love, of which the Christ in the West and Shri Krishna in the East are the great leaders.

In dealing with others, you will not be able to separate your happiness from theirs, and this will lead you to become a teacher of the ignorant, a helper of the weak, a producer of something that will make for the greater happiness of mankind. If you pursue knowledge, it will be for the sake of love; if you work hard, it will be inspired by love. It will not be knowledge that leads you to love, but love that leads you to knowledge and activity. You can test your fundamental character by asking yourself whether love leads to the other two. If it does, you will know that you belong predominantly to this line.

It is not necessary to say much about the virtue of love, for it has been taught with marvelous perfection in the *Bhagavad-Gita* of the Hindus and in the *New Testament* of the Christian Bible, as well as in many other places. We need but note that perfect love can never be wounded because it forgets self utterly in thinking of others' outlook upon life.

Love is, however, a path full of dangers, when it is not accompanied by strength of will and well-balanced understanding. In its rudimentary and very imperfect form, it often leads to acts of kindness done simply to remove one's own distress produced by sympathy at the sight of others suffering, as for example in the case of a person who gives money to a professional beggar in order to remove his horrid presence. This kind of reaction is provoked by many social defects which sensitive and refined people try to hide away and forget—for example, the dreadful poverty found all over the world and the terrible conditions in prisons. In such cases the strength of will and understanding of life required to deal with the root problems of lack of love in society are often insufficient, even where love is strong. Love must come forward with all its bodyguard of understanding and determined work before it can really fulfill its mission in the world.

It is characteristic of this type that, in the conflict of duties, a person will often decide upon kindness in preference to truth, and will weakly refrain from responsibilities which involve decisions that may lead to acts which on the surface may not seem kind. Such a one may save himself from this dangerous error by realizing that love involves a mingling in all life, and that in the long run truth is a great power for human unity.

14
INTUITION

Anyone who is developing along the line of will finds that as he proceeds that quality of will brings him nearer to freedom, first of all by controlling the thoughts, emotions, and actions of his personality. Similarly, on the line that we have now to consider, the same three parts of the personality are brought under the direction of knowledge that is so swift and sure that the only names that we can give to it are *intuition* and *insight*.

Eastern philosophy has always maintained that the thinking mind, which is part of our personality, is an exceedingly imperfect and undeveloped thing and that its range is extremely limited. This aspect of the mind is only an instrument usable for a particular purpose, just as one would take a boat to travel on the sea or an automobile to travel over land. And just as one would not try to travel over all seas in one's little boat or over all lands in one's car, so we need not try to gain all knowledge by means of the physical senses and the ratiocinating mind. The actions that we can perform with our bodies are few, but the will can apply them in an infinite variety of ways. So also the knowledge that we can gain is relatively little, but intuition can make it infinitely significant. Pieces of knowledge are innumerable, and you can go on adding one to another indefinitely. But when the intuition works, with its direct vision of the truth, it irradiates the mind and illuminates the whole field of knowledge.

The yoga philosophy states that there are three principal modes of gaining knowledge—by direct vision, by reasoning, and by the testimony of credible witnesses. It regards the last two of these as mere makeshifts. Mental life cannot forever remain so imperfect and indirect. But, as the higher mind grows, a faculty of direct mental perception will replace the present clumsy and halting methods which are shaping what is almost a rudimentary organ. All this bears out the general principle that in the spiritual life it is quality, not quantity, that is important.

In writing on education I have pointed out that the mind should be sharpened as a tool, not filled as a museum, and this is a valid method when we are dealing with the personal mind of a growing child. But when we are striving to realize that higher mind whose faculty is intuition, I would rather say that the mind should be treated as a lamp to be kept clean and bright, so that light may be steady and pure within it and may shine outward upon all things. As we go through the dark places of life, they are lighted up from within ourselves. It is infinitely more important that we should attend to the perfection of that light than that we should store huge quantities of memories of facts and experience, most of which we shall never need.

On this line of development, the ideal is realization, the virtue is truth, and the instrument of progress is understanding. It leads people to become philosophers and to see the principles underlying all forms. It gives great power for abstract reasoning. In the life of the world, joined with an active disposition, it gives great adaptability, for its owner can see the same essential in many forms and will find a value in everything that has been evolved by the Divine Mind in nature.

The danger of this third line appears when the will power and the love nature are not strong enough to prompt one to action, and the person tends to become a spectator of life, keenly interested in understanding it but not eager to mingle with it. He must use his understanding to develop the qualities which he lacks.

The chief practice on this line will be that in which one learns to calm the lower mind while keeping up the activity of the intelligence, so as to receive intuitions in the perfectly controlled personality. For this the later chapters of my book *Concentration*, particularly that on "Contemplation," provide a course.

15
IMAGINATION

There is one great mystery of life that no intellect can understand—the way in which thought and matter are connected, or rather related. What is the nature of that peculiar harmony by which consciousness and matter are related in a marvelous series of correspondences, so that for every thought there is a corresponding and obedient action and form, and every action and form in the outer world has the power to awaken ideas in the mind? Nobody can say. But there are minds specially tuned to this divine magic that fills the world, minds that take delight in a constant vision and use of the relation between spiritual and material things.

Looking at the scenes of earth, full of changing color, sound, and form, such people see not matter but the play of a Divine Mind, comparable to the human mind but infinitely richer in powers and in spiritual capacities. As we may see mountain tops mirrored in a still lake, so they see in the qualities of this world the play of soul powers of will, love, and thought. What to others looks like matter is to them the expression of soul. Conversely, they clothe every thought in color or sound, and by their vivid and spontaneous imagination they relate every spiritual or abstract idea to a never-ending series of corresponding forms. They always see the one in the many and the many in the one, and there opens for them a special line of creative activity in which the imagination plays the greatest part.

The language of this type of people is full of imagery, for they constantly see likenesses in the most diverse things. Their reasoning is full of analogy. Their art is full of suggestion. Their actions tend to be dramatic. They realize outward life by imitation. In all they do they are not thinking of precise effects in the material world but of the representation in life of the wonderful things that they contact in what to others is but the dreamland of the soul. In their creative work they use imagination above all other faculties.

There is in them a harmony between soul and personality, such that the former can never leave the latter alone, so that the personality is often torn in conflict between its response to soul impulses and its smooth obedience to the environment in which its lot is cast.

I have related the words *magic* and *imagination* to this type for a special reason. Magic was never concerned so much with scientific investigation or intuitional observation as with the sudden perception of relationships and correspondences and the storing of these in memory. And memory itself—strong in this type of person—is the greatest of magic, transcending all limitations of space and time.

If you belong to this type, you can range over the whole field of human experience. By imagination you can put yourself in the position of others, and find a means also for expressing what is perceived and felt at the level of the soul.

16
INVESTIGATION

If you belong to one of the first three types already mentioned, in which will or love or understanding leads your forces of character, you are one of those who unconsciously seek perfection and happiness by retreating within yourself. The use of these faculties is in itself a delight and an inspiration, and the outer forms in which they express themselves are secondary, just as the apparatus of physical culture—the bars, the bells, the clubs—are to the athlete only a casual means to his end of self-development.

But you may belong to another great class of people who seek happiness and perfection by advancing without. If they are following a spiritual path, they drink in all the divine nourishment by devotion to God in the external world—in the obedience to his law that marks the scientific mind; in the prostration before his love that characterizes the religious devotee; and in the pursuit of his beauty that is the essence of all true art. All these are forms of faith in God as being in the external world and of that reverence and worship by means of which one absorbs into himself the divine qualities. Most people are not aware of what is going on beneath the surface current of their lives. You must find out where your allegiance lies and then encourage and develop it.

All progress means an ever-increasing self-conscious association with God, the omniscient, omnipotent, omnipresent. We have seen that will can become highly developed only when it is at one with the universal moral law of justice. So knowledge can only increase through a spirit of truth that renders unhesitating obedience to the laws of the world which it studies. A thinking mind that had not behind it a hidden religion as inexplicable faith in the intelligibility or understandability of the whole world, a mind that presumed to imagine that there was something wrong with the laws of nature and the laws of thought, would bring its own progress to a standstill. Consciously or unconsciously, men of will and of knowledge bow in faith to something greater than themselves—that is to say, greater morally and mentally.

If you belong to this fifth type of development,

your leading activity will be that of the investigating mind, eager for knowledge, confident that whatever knowledge is found will prove useful to humanity, and instinctively obedient to the laws governing all forms—the arrangement of the world made by the Divine Mind. You will have confidence in the outer world and belief that will lead you to the truth. One of your strongest virtues will be accuracy of observation and record-keeping and carefulness in classification.

I know a great man of this type who was so meticulously accurate that he would insist that all letters be folded to fit their envelopes precisely, and that the stamp be put on the envelope perfectly straight and about the same distance from the top and side edges. This showed an alliance of the fifth type and the seventh (that of beauty), which we shall presently study. It might seem that this accuracy was a waste of time, but in fact it represents a form of allegiance to truth that develops great soul power.

Investigation allied with the will to create produces the experimenter and inventor in all fields of progress. People of this type have done much to increase the scope of human experience by giving added power to our senses and activities.

Like all strong virtues, investigation may prove to be the core of a vice. The mind seeks means for the removal of human ills, and relying upon the guidance of investigation (observation and experiment) alone, it disregards our best feelings and our sense of beauty. Thus in combating disease it runs to vivisection and other inhumane practices, instead of looking for harmless means. The ancient Greeks, full of love of beauty and philosophical understanding, show us by contrast the error of our modern ways. When the two methods of love and understanding are combined, we may expect a great perfection of human personal life.

17
DEVOTION

Every religion has spoken of the uplifting power of divine grace. Each has explained that grace works in the soul, cleansing, uplifting, strengthening, only in response to that voluntary devotion which is emotional worship. This devotion is a response to the love of God for his world, as the eager investigation of the scientific mind is a self-developing response to his law. Just as surely as investigation with a pure desire for truth develops the mind of the searcher (so that it comes ever nearer in nature and condition to the truth behind all things), so does the constant hymn of praise and prayer of the devoted worshipper nourish his own mind with the emotional beauty of its ideal God.

If you are a devotee and love of God is the leader of the forces of your soul, your devotion is an open channel between your soul and God in the world.

Your devotion is therefore a definite faculty of the soul, like thinking or willing or loving. As humans have a distinct and unquestionable power to think, so we have a distinct power to worship. Just as the physical eye opens to take in sights of the world of sense, so does devotion open the soul to take in the things of the spiritual world.

We may say that a plant grows up through the soil and into the air, through the material devices enfolded in its germ and seed. But it is equally true that the latent powers in the seed are drawn upwards by the enticement and nourishment of the sun. There is far more evolution by attraction from above than by propulsion from beneath. It is not sufficiently recognized that the evolution of creatures very largely depends upon their association with superiors. Domestic animals are uplifted by association with man to a higher state of intelligence, a sense of right and wrong, and a degree of faithful affection which are sometimes as good as human, though narrow in their scope. Even in animal societies where one species is often at war with another, it is frequently the case that the battle with a superior develops capacity and strength. Nature is full of creatures that have adapted to dangers from stronger species, such as the insects that are camouflaged to resemble plant parts. Some biologists would insist that the development of the human brain to its present pitch of efficiency is due to man's weaker physical nature and absence of natural weapons, which have forced him to depend upon cunning rather than strength or swiftness. It is a general rule throughout life that progress comes mainly through help from above. Humanity acknowledges this by its reverence to the God idea, conceived in different degrees of crudity or refinement, as it has occurred among all peoples.

The man who follows the path of devotion—as for example the Hindu who repeats the thousand and one names of the Divine Being, with meditation on their meaning, and who dedicates himself to the service of that Being—is definitely drawing nearer in qualities to his ideal. The use of hymns of praise and prayer is not that God may enjoy our adulation but that, in an entirely receptive mood, we may have our attention fixed upon our best conception of the Divine Being.

The two chief dangers for this devotional type are inactivity and thoughtlessness. In contemplation of what is so far above, one sometimes forgets the world of duty among one's fellows and fails to apply, and to understand how to apply, those growing virtues which have been absorbed from the world of God. It is easy to forget that smaller world of personal thought and action and love where one's self is god—the willer, the thinker, the actor. The result of this thoughtlessness and inactivity, when it is carried too far, is the strangulation even of the devotional life, for life is not feeling alone. Just as activity and feeling are necessary to understanding, so is studious practice of virtues in life necessary to their pure absorption through the avenues of emotion. It is, of course, inevitable that in the early days of practice the character is ill balanced, and therefore thought may be crude and activity awkward. Devotion lacking in intelligence may march along narrow and injurious paths of superstition, sentimentality, and intolerance. But these are errors which will correct themselves with growth and will leave in the end a perfect character attuned to the divine grace of all life.

18
LOVE OF BEAUTY

God is recognizable and approachable in the world not only by investigation into the True and yearning for the Good. He is equally attainable by means of every sense in the material world, as the Beauty in all beautiful things. There can be no question that all virtue can enter into us through our contemplation of God as Beauty.

If love of beauty is your leading quality, the pursuit will awaken all the powers of your soul, unite them on account of its omnipresence in you, and lead your whole character on to superhuman perfection. You may recognize your type by the ease with which you respond to the beautiful.

To stand and gaze up with reverence at the mighty Himalayan mountains with their snowy peaks is to drink in something of the strength and purity of the God that they represent in the world of sense. To contemplate with reverent gratitude the glowing splendor of the sunrise is to assimilate something of the peace and splendor of God that we have witnessed, so that we have become richer than before. The seed of life has taken true nourishment from such appreciation and has grown nearer to the perfect sun of life.

Indeed, the whole world is the book of God written for our reading, so that we may know him with a living knowledge. Our ability to read this book is cultivated by the deliberate opening up of our nature in grateful appreciation of beauty. The God idea in us would be crude and feeble without these grand representations in the material world. Therefore, a person who reverences the divine neither in personified form nor in the abstract but manifest as beauty in the universe, who strives everywhere to see and feel that beauty, is also by such devotion developing the divine attributes. He is realizing God within himself more and more. This seventh type of human progress by response to beauty does not lend itself well to description and explanation, but each one who has had real experience of it in any degree will know what is meant.

People in whom devotion to God as beauty predominates in the character generally follow that outward philosophy of life that leads one to live in the present without undue regard to past or future.

People of this type do not attempt to penetrate into the mysteries of fate nor trouble much about the past. They are the true Epicureans, who feel that the feast of life has been well laid out before them on the table of nature. It is theirs to enjoy in fullest happiness, so that—through absence of anxiety and through perfect trust in the healing and creative powers of nature—they may grow in love and beauty, like the lilies of the field that sow not, neither spin.

Beauty and love, flowing into such people from their constant ideal, gradually come to control and guide the entire personality, all thoughts, emotions and actions, forming the prevailing mood. These lovers of beauty learn to see greatness in everything, not only in what is strikingly beautiful or labeled so in conventional thought, but throughout the entire world. They learn to read not only the large print of the book of life, but also the smaller print that escapes the attention of most people.

The last three types mentioned, in whom the scientific, the devotional, and the artistic spirit predominate, have one strong quality in common—that of love of God expressed in something external. When combined with strong devotion, the religion of the devotee will express itself in forms of religious beauty—particularly in artistic ceremonial. There is a clear distinction between the art that expresses beauty and that which, while quite unbeautiful in itself, suggests to the beholder the beauty that he conceives in his own mind. This is to be seen in India, where the most ignorant of the people are yet so well developed in imagination and the magical sense of the fourth type that the sight even of an ungainly image or picture of Shri Krishna will call up deep devotion, full of the vision of God's beauty. Very often to the Western Christian observer, such an image or picture seems grotesque. The Christian may belong to the seventh type and love the beauty of God expressed, not suggested, in beautiful forms of the outer world, while the art of the fourth type is often full of symbol and imagery.

The quality of the seventh type was strongly shown in the Greek love of beauty, which was allied with philosophy, so that the Greeks not only loved art but also had a reason for their love. They clearly saw its quality of adherence to the Divine when they argued that the great artist was one who saw more clearly than others the beauty of the forms created by the Divine Mind, and was able to isolate various elements of that beauty and express them in sculptured or architectural or other form to the less developed vision of ordinary men. Allegiance to the divine beauty in the world was one of the greatest virtues of the artist.

Beauty has also a peculiar quality of stability, which it imparts to its devotees in the form of peace, a kind of living beauty in the soul. It is the repose of perfect action and also peace within the soul.

IV

Seeking Happiness

19
THE EMOTIONS

As your emotions relate you in feeling to the world around you, it is desirable to study a little more fully the play of your emotions, which are in part based upon judgment of the object of emotion. The two grand emotions are liking and disliking—in stronger words, love and hate—and these are again divisible into sets of three, according to the circumstances. Consider the emotional attitude of ourselves to God; we feel reverence, devotion, worship. The relation of one person to another should be one of friendship or brotherliness. That of God to man is benevolence.

These three types of relationships appear in different degrees in all our human encounters. I have at least a faint judgment of everyone I meet that he is my superior, equal, or inferior, at least with regard to the subject that matters at the moment. According to this judgment or fancy or supposition, as the case may be, my emotion changes. My liking becomes some degree of admiration, respect, or reverence towards the superior, of friendliness towards the equal, or kindness towards the inferior. The three forms of dislike would be fear, anger, and active pride.

Liking seeks to unite, disliking to separate the subject and object of emotion, either in material fact or by reducing or increasing the gulf of inequality. True benevolence seeks to raise the object of its compassion to a condition of equality; it is no true kindness which leaves the recipient with an added sense of his own dependence and inferiority in some respect. (Here is to be discovered the cause of the germ of hatred that tends to infect the soul against the demonstrative giver who has helped us much but robbed us of independence, self-respect, and true liberty. It is amazing how many people secretly hate their benefactors.) Similarly, true reverence tends to lift its possessor towards the object of worship, and love equalizes the parties to it more and more by affectionate give and take. The following table shows the relationships of the principal emotions:

	LOVE (Attraction)	HATE (Repulsion)
To inferiors	Kindness	Superciliousness
	Benevolence	Insolence
	Compassion	Arrogance
	Self-sacrifice	Cruel pride
To equals	Friendliness	Dislike
	Affection	Hostility
	Brotherliness	Anger
	Love	Ferocity
To superiors	Admiration	Timidity
	Respect	Fear
	Reverence	Horror
	Worship	Terror

The emotions of love are spiritual. They accompany expansion of the soul in the wider life of others—giving without stint and taking without resentment—and are thus progressive emotions. Those of hate are material, tending to expand the life in bodily possessions and position not held for the sake of others, excluding others—taking without consideration, and giving with deep resentment—and are thus retrograde emotions.

In the work of character building, it is of the greatest importance to give up the emotions that are retrograde, not by destroying them and making the emotional life weak and colorless, but by taking any quality on the side of hatred and converting it into its equivalent quality on the side of love. This is done by a triple process: first, by imagining scenes in which the hateful quality is expressed by you; second, by turning the little key mentioned in Chapter 6 and so transmuting the scene to one in which your love emotion appears; and third, by practicing in the outer world what you have already gone over in imagination.

One or two examples will make this transmutation process somewhat more intelligible. If you find pride and a sense of superiority rising in you at the sight of one who is weak or ignorant or unlucky, you know that this can only appear on account of selfishness. You are thinking about your own accomplishments. But transfer your consciousness to the other person and try to look upon the world from his eyes, forgetting yourself, and your pride will be converted to sympathy or compassion. You will find the opposite case somewhat more difficult, but exactly the same principle applies. If you find yourself in the presence of a tyrant or bully who has power to injure you, hatred may rise within you in the form of fear. The turn of the key will show you that there is something that you can obtain through that person—there is some little thing at least for you to admire, or he would not be in his present position towards you. It will become apparent in our chapter on the fundamental vices that what we usually call emotional vice results from too great a development of one quality at the expense of others. You will realize that the man is not positively vicious, but that it is some strength of his that brings out his defects.

In all this work of filling your life with progressive emotions, you will of course have continual falls, and there will be a constant temptaion to try to avoid all circumstances which are too difficult. It is easy to go and live in a forest and from that seclusion feel good will toward all mankind; but it is another matter if you have to take your part in the struggle of life, perhaps with a family dependent upon you. While it is not advisable for anyone to take upon his shoulders a burden that is too heavy for him to carry, it is undoubtedly true that the one who shoulders his burden is the one who will develop strength. Though he may fall a hundred times in the beginning, it does not matter in the least. What is important is to get up again every time.

The question of success and failure in this matter must always take into account the ratio between success and difficulty or temptation. Virtue or strength is not a question of absolutes; it is relative to the load which has to be borne. At the same

113

time, it is advisable to recognize the manner in which emotional strength grows by repetition of effort within reasonable limits, as do the muscles of the physical body by repetition of exercises. Every time you harbor an emotion of the selfish or retrograde class, you weaken yourself for future struggles. Every time you evolve one of the spiritual or unselfish class, you add some permanent strength which will make all future struggles easier.

This study of the science of the sympathetic and antipathetic emotions is as definite and usable as a science of material things, such as chemistry or physics. It is knowledge which, when applied, brings certain results.

It will be found that all those virtues which are prescribed by the various religions fall into the first of our classes. People often feel some confusion and some hopelessness on account of the great variety of virtues required, but a little study will show that they all fall very conveniently into our table. Take for example the sixteenth discourse of the *Bhagavad-Gita*, where there is a list of the qualities that raise man towards divinity. The following is a translation of the first three verses:

Courage, cleanness of life, steadfast attachment to wisdom, generosity, self-control and sacrifice, study of what concerns yourself, honesty, harm-

114

lessness, truth, absence of anger, letting go, peacefulness, absence of backbiting, sympathy for living beings, uncovetousness, gentleness, modesty, absence of fickleness, vigor, forgiveness, fortitude, purity, absence of envy and conceit—these are his who is born with the divine qualities.

If you desire to follow up this approach to the study of the emotions in fuller detail, you will find a lucid treatment of the subject in the latter part of Annie Besant's *A Study in Consciousness* (Adyar: Theosophical Publishing House, 1972).

20
THE FUNDAMENTAL VICES

There are in human character no positive vices or excrescences to be removed. The three fundamental vices—laziness, thoughtlessness, and selfishness—and all other vices that spring from them are essentially negative, the result of the absence of their corresponding virtues. Laziness is the absence of courage and self-control; thoughtlessness is the absence of truth; and selfishness is the absence of love.

When a vice appears to be positive, it takes its positive quality from a virtue with which it is associated and which gives it all its strength for evil. Thus strongly developed activity and courage without love and truth would produce a dangerous person, but an idle person lacking courage would be too feeble to be really vicious. Similarly, a person full of love and activity but lacking judgment and thought would be dangerous to those around him, especially if he were in public life. He may, for example, rouse feelings which would lead to public disturbance if, on account of his lack of interest in the truth and the laws of life, he has not given a matter sufficient thought. His defects become dangerous vices when allied to his positive virtue.

It is, therefore, a cardinal principle in the science of character building (and of education of the young) that there shall be no repression, for every force is a virtue and is valuable. In producing a perfect character, the method of the sculptor will never do. Of the three modes of producing a form, that of the sculptor, the builder, the gardener, the last comes nearest to the method to be adopted. But even in creating a garden there is too much harshness, too much external determination, for a satisfactory treatment of a seed so delicate and yet so potent as the human soul.

The correct treatment of what appear to be positive vices is education in the corresponding virtues. If a person is brave but selfish, we do not want to repress his bravery but to develop his affection for his fellows by suitable environment and stimulus. If, therefore, in training yourself, you find what appears to be a positive vice, study it in relation to the three fundamental vices of laziness, thoughtlessness and selfishness, discover your defect, and level up the ground of your character. Do not repress or destroy. It is very easy to be good and colorless, yet the old saying is strictly true: "The greater the sinner, the greater the saint."

There is some consolation in this idea in that we are saved from the paradoxical belief that a good God creates evil men. There are no evil men but only imperfect ones, and every bit of experience tends to the development of at least one of the three fundamental virtues. The distinction between virtues and vices is relative, not absolute, and defects of human character are only imperfections and disproportions. This explains the statement made by Shri Krishna in the tenth chapter of the *Bhagavad-Gita*, where, in the midst of a long list of the glories of the Creator as manifested in all the beautiful things of life, he suddenly says: "I am the gambling of the cheat."

The positive vice is of great utility. A selfish man may have vigor and courage, which make his defect a vice, and he plunges into injurious action. This inevitably reacts upon himself, even in the material world, and brings him suffering of some kind, which gradually awakens in him a sympathetic feeling for the sufferings of others. Then love develops, which he would not have acquired without that experience.

It is not usual for moralists to perceive these

118

root causes of vice. They usually fulminate against the more obvious social vices—very well summed up as lust, anger, and greed—and an attempt is made to battle against these without appropriate weapons. The almost invariable result is failure.

Vices must be meditated upon in the light of the three fundamental vices, and all the vigor of life that they contain, which gives them their savor, must be retained, but allied with new developments. Thus the greed of the unscrupulous and vigorous millionaire will gradually change its face, not by indiscriminate distribution of his fortune and retiring to a monastery, but by his using the vice for the prosperity of his neighbors. Then, as he finds the joy of life in seeing their happiness, his newborn sympathies will gradually percolate into all his smaller dealings and purify his life. When his services are employed for the common good, he will be a potent force for the benefit of all.

Behind this analysis of virtues and vices lies an important philosophical and spiritual truth. There is no vice in man, and the perfect man approaches our highest conception of the character of God. What does distinguish our degrees of imperfection is the fact that we are always losing and forgetting ourselves. We are deluded into accepting a false personality, like a woman who has never known her own form by its appearance in a mirror. She is suddenly brought before a fattening and distorting mirror and, imagining herself to be truly portrayed, acts according to the delusion.

We always have some inkling of our real spiritual selves. This leaves a seed of discontent within us, which will not allow us to be satisfied for long with the distorted personality and its apparent needs. You have only to analyze your conception of yourself to see how utterly external and ludicrous it is.

In modern life often the opinions of neighbors provide most of the clay and paint for this absurd idol. We hear what our friends say about us—that we are ugly or handsome, foolish or wise, ignorant or learned, competent or incompetent, significant or insignificant. Out of these mirror images as the years of childhood and youth roll by, we gradually compact a whole mass of varied and often inconsistent material around that center of consciousness which is the spiritual self. All true effort in the building of character penetrates beneath this personality to the realization of our own spiritual self. We develop powers in our character so that they shine through the personality and change it, and we become ourselves, even in this mortal and delusive life. As we act with spiritual motives in this life of the personality, we *are* the immortal Higher Self.

21
ULTIMATE AIMS

One of the difficulties of self-determined progress is that you cannot see very far into the future, and the future that you now decide upon must be tainted with your present imperfection of judgment. It is not possible to draw up in advance every detail of your building of character, as an architect would specify beforehand the detailed features of a house to be built. Nevertheless, general principles of progress require that your building be done deliberately, as in the building of a house. For a house, you would take each piece of material, prepare it or shape it, and then carefully fix it in its proper place. That must be done also in building character. You have the satisfaction, however, that as the work proceeds the plan can be constantly altered and improved, so that its final form will be more glorious than anything now imaginable.

You must realize that no barrier to this work is to be contemplated. Many people imagine that death will put an end to their work. But in this process death does not count at all, as it is of practically no importance. Whatever the future may be, it depends upon the present and is bound to lead ever onward and upward according to spiritual principles. These spiritual principles are as clearly discernible to us in the physical world as they are likely to be in any other. Indeed, when we are true to ourselves, we are spiritual beings even now. What there is of spirituality in us has unfolded from the seed within us that is destined to carry on our conscious evolution to inconceivable perfections and powers. Character grows only from within, though it absorbs what it needs from without.

Our ignorance of our future is not so great as it at first may seem, for there are several very distinct guideposts such as we find, for example, in the chapter on emotions, and guiding stars such as the glimpses of intuitions described in Chapter 3. By noting the ideal that you have in your best moments when the mind is free from agitation, and aiming at that ideal at other times when it may be difficult to keep it in view, you certainly will evoke from within yourself what is best, and also absorb what is best from the outer world.

There are three lines of human progress—knowledge, love, and work. It is impossible to overestimate the value for practical purposes of knowing of these. They point the direct road to the transition from material to spiritual desires.

There is no human being void of desire, but desires fall into two distinct classes, the material and the spiritual. Material desire leads to pleasure and pain, both of which are transient. Spiritual desires lead to happiness, an attribute of the Divine, which is permanent or infinite. For this reason happiness is one of the best guides to progress. When there is real, permanent progress, there is happiness or joy. When you feel pain, there is something wrong with you, not with the world.

Pain checks and corrects. It is only a reaction from one of your positive vices, and its business is to tell you, very forcibly if need be, that you are going off the right track. It demands that you shall think, love, or act, as the case may require. It insists upon your using your powers for spiritual ends. Pain is thus a friend to save you from any possibility of a downward path. Even your pleasures soon pass away, and if you persist in them after the material desire has faded, they will turn to pain. It is wisdom, therefore, not to shun these things with any sort of fear, but to draw from pleasure and pain the lessons that they can teach, or rather to accept from them the guidance that they have to offer. It may be that you suffer pain because you have been lazy or thoughtless or selfish; now is the time to find out which of these it is and set yourself on the right road for the future.

With happiness the case is different. Happiness arises out of the exercise of all our three qualities—in other words, from work done with thought or love. Take the case of the unselfish artist; his work never bores him. Or the case of a scientist pursuing his thought for the benefit of mankind; he enjoys happiness, not pleasure, and happiness never falls away. Take the case of the farmer who toils in the fields, applying his knowledge for the benefit of his family; he enjoys happiness. There are thousands of avenues of happiness in human life, but in every case it will be found that it is the fruit of spiritual desires, which require the union of work, thought, and love.

22
THE GREAT LAW

It has been made clear in the earlier chapters of this book that we cannot get on without faith. Sometimes it is the faith which makes us place our trust in nature, like the lilies of the field; sometimes it makes us trust in our own intelligence, working in the universe of invariable law which is perfectly intelligible; sometimes it makes us trust in the triumph of right in a universe instinct with moral law.

Long before we understand the intelligibility of the universe, we exercise reason, and long before we see how justice is done, we realize by spiritual perception that the spiritual law has produced it. Everyone has a not unnatural desire for justice, and the great law which governs the world provides for its satisfaction, as it does for the satisfaction of the intellectual nature and the emotions.

There is perfect justice in all outer happenings between people and between man and God. We must not estimate justice by our feelings but by what is best for the person concerned.

It is, therefore, desirable in the practice of character building to accept all things that come as from the hand of God. If an illness or a great difficulty arises, do not resent it and wish it were not there, but realize that it is the thing that you most need, or in this moral world it would not have come to you. You must face the situation with vigor and courage, with thought and with a cheerful and loving heart. Overcome it if you think it should be overcome; submit to it if you think that is the best course for the development of character. But in every case look it straight in the face and determine that you will get from it what it has the power to give.

On the other hand, take care when things that are pleasant come your way—wealth, influence, praise or fame, good health, beauty. These are as dangerous as the difficulties and no more desirable, unless you have the strength of character (in all three departments) to cope with them without injury to yourself and others. One who would tread this path must realize the delusive nature of pleasure and pain, and he will find—though it must sound strange to those who have not yet experienced it—that there is abundant happiness to be derived from both.

Avoiding resentment is therefore the key to success. It is a general principle that anything in the nature of agitation obliterates the powers of character as long as it lasts, and resentment is a form of agitation of the most persistent type. It is true that there are things to be battled against, but not with hatred, anxiety, and resentment. It often happens that our enemy is in reality our best friend. There is nothing in the whole world that cannot be used for the development of character. Believe, therefore, in the triumph of right, and lead the spiritual life even in this world.

One way to avoid resentment is to abstain from blaming others. Praise is also a very doubtful activity, for it implies that you consider yourself a judge, and really all praise of others is essentially self-praise. But blame is more dangerous because it generally produces more agitation. You get annoyed because other people do not do what you think they ought to do. Intellectual criticism of others is useful, because it is part of the study of human nature. It is always safe to study those who differ from you, for they have probably acquired something that you have overlooked. But the habit of emotional criticism wastes the energy that you need for your own work.

In the life of Yudhishtira, one of the Hindu epic heroes, there is an excellent illustration of these principles. King Yudhishtira was a very righteous man but a little weak in some directions. When he was challenged to a game of dice by his uncle Shakuni, he did not like to refuse the game because that would have been contrary to the conventions of his class and time. He grew excited with the gambling, and Shakuni, who was a clever trickster, led him on until his kingdom and everything else that he possessed was lost. This led to a dispute which ended in the Great War of the Bharatas and brought upon Yudhishtira the most terrible trials.

After the war when Yudhishtira had lost all his brothers and friends, he wandered in a lonely place with no one but a dog whom he had made his friend. A Deva appeared to him and told him that it was time for him to come away and enjoy the bliss of high heaven. But, obstinate through all arguments and pleadings, he refused to leave the animal that depended upon him. At this, the dog turned into a glorious Deva. Yudhishtira was declared to have shown great strength of character, and all three ascended to the high heaven.

Yudhishtira looked round for his brothers and friends, and not finding them, he insisted that it was impossible for him to enjoy the bliss of heaven until he was assured that those he loved were enjoying it too. His companions led him to a darkened place where he could hear the groans of his brothers. When he learned where they were, he refused to leave the abode of misery and preferred to remain to try to comfort them.

Once more the scene changed, and Yudhishtira found himself enjoying the bliss of heaven with those whom he had loved. Yudhishtira had been transformed from a good, weak man into a good, strong man through the gambling of Shakuni, the cheat. As Shri Krishna said: "I am the gambling of the cheat."

It is time to give up wishing, which implies failure, and to learn to see truly and apply both will and love. When that is done, the whole universe will change its face towards you, and it will not be long before you enter a higher and more spiritual state of being, to which our human condition is but an early apprenticeship.